Strategic Studies Institute
and
U.S. Army War College Press

RUSSIA AFTER PUTIN

Richard J. Krickus

May 2014

*****

Comments pertaining to this report are invited and should be forwarded to: Director, Strategic Studies Institute and U.S. Army War College Press, U.S. Army War College, 47 Ashburn Drive, Carlisle, PA 17013-5010.

*****

This manuscript was funded by the U.S. Army War College External Research Associates Program. Information on this program is available on our website, *www.StrategicStudies Institute.army.mil*, at the Opportunities tab.

*****

*****

The Strategic Studies Institute and U.S. Army War College Press publishes a monthly email newsletter to update the national security community on the research of our analysts, recent and forthcoming publications, and upcoming conferences sponsored by the Institute. Each newsletter also provides a strategic commentary by one of our research analysts. If you are interested in receiving this newsletter, please subscribe on the SSI website at *www.StrategicStudiesInstitute.army.mil/newsletter*.

FOREWORD

As the United States reassesses relations with Russia and develops doctrine that addresses a turbulent security environment, Dr. Richard J. Krickus addresses a brace of pivotal questions that have a bearing on the future of Vladimir Putin and his Power Vertical. Are Putin's days numbered as many Russian watchers predict and what will Russia look like after he leaves the Kremlin? Toward this end, Krickus assesses four plausible scenarios. They include first, Status Quo, depicting the major geo-political features of Russia today; second, Stalin Lite that embraces most of the characteristics of a police state; third, The Western Path to Development that reflects pluralistic phenomenon associated with a "normal" European country; and fourth, Russia in Chaos, an outcome that anticipates the virtual disintegration of Russia as we know it today.

The plausibility of these scenarios varies with a move toward Stalin Lite most likely — some would argue that we are already there — a pluralistic Russia less so, and a Russia consumed in chaos least likely. In his assessment of all four outcomes, Dr. Krickus considers their domestic and international implications and dwells specifically upon what bearing they might have upon the capacity of the United States and Russia to collaborate in meeting common security problems: coping with international terrorism; stemming the proliferation of weapons of mass destructrion; and resolving violent internal struggles that have profound regional and international implications like the Syrian Civil War.

Dr. Krickus concludes that, in spite of many obstacles, the leadership in Washington and Moscow must find ways to address security threats of this nature even as the United States rebalances toward Asia. Moreover, he agrees with prominent statesmen like Zbigniew Brzezinski and Henry Kissinger that ultimately, Russia must be integrated into a Euro-Atlantic security system.

The unexpected turbulent events of September 2013 that have resulted in a United Nations resolution compelling Syria to surrender its chemical weapons and to restart the Geneva negotiations to find a diplomatic resolution to the Syrian crisis offers evidence that a partnership, even if limited and fragile, is plausible. A major consideration of the U.S. national security establishment must be how to operationalize the partnership.

For all intents and purposes, the United States and Russia now have taken responsibility for resolving the Syrian crisis and in the process have reached a new chapter in the reset of relations. If they succeed in finding a diplomatic solution to it, further cooperation on other shared security concerns will follow. If not, they will take a turn for the worse.

Douglas C. Lovelace, Jr.

DOUGLAS C. LOVELACE, JR.
Director
Strategic Studies Institute and
   U.S. Army War College Press

ABOUT THE AUTHOR

RICHARD J. KRICKUS is a Distinguished Professor Emeritus at the University of Mary Washington and has held the Oppenheimer Chair for Warfighting Strategy at the U.S. Marine Corps University. Previously, he cofounded The National Center for Urban Ethnic Affairs in Washington, DC, and in the early-1970s began conducting research on the Union of Soviet Socialist Republics' "nationalities question." In this connection, he began to write about popular unrest among the people of Lithuania. In 1990, Sajudis, the Lithuanian popular front movement, invited him to serve as an international monitor for the first democratic election conducted in Soviet Lithuania. Dr. Krickus has offered testimony to the Senate Foreign Relations Committee and has lectured at the U.S. Foreign Service Institute, the Polish Foreign Ministry, the European Commission, and other domestic and foreign venues on the Soviet Union/Russia, the Baltic countries, NATO, and Kaliningrad. He has published widely on these issues for academic and policy-oriented journals as well as various newspapers, including *The Washington Post*, *The Chicago Sun-Times*, the *Los Angeles Times*, and *The Wall Street Journal Europe*. For 8 years, Dr. Krickus wrote a column on world affairs for *Lietuvos Rytas*, Lithuania's leading national daily. He has appeared as a commentator on Soviet-Russian affairs on U.S. radio and television on numerous occasions. He is the author of a number of books, including: *Pursuing the American Dream*; *The Superpowers in Crisis*; *Showdown: The Lithuanian Rebellion and the Break-Up of the Soviet Empire*; *The Kaliningrad Question*; *Iron Troikas: The New Threat from the East*; *Medvedev's Plan: Giving Russia a Voice but Not a Veto in a New European Secu-*

rity System; and *The Afghanistan Question and the Reset in U.S.-Russian Relations*. Dr. Krickus holds a B.A. in government from the College of William and Mary, an M.A. in international affairs from the University of Massachusetts, and a Ph.D. in comparative politics from Georgetown University.

SUMMARY

Note: This research was completed in the fall of 2013, which was obviously prior to the recent crisis in Crimea and Ukraine.

In 1999, after Boris Yeltsin appointed Vladimir Putin Prime Minister, the former Russian Secret Service (KGB) agent pledged to create a powerful state at home capable of projecting Russia's influence abroad. He spoke favorably about democracy but soon indicated by his actions that political authority would be concentrated in his hands alone, although he surrounded himself with a medley of supporters: members of the security services and military — collectively known as the Siloviki — business tycoons, high-level government officials, and members of criminal organizations. The state's resurrection — what became known as the Power Vertical — was made possible largely through surging gas and oil revenues and Putin's tight hold over the reins of power. The revenues that they produced, in turn, expanded the urban middle class, and provided jobs for those working in Soviet-era enterprises and entitlements for retirees. In return, Putin enjoyed unprecedented approval in the eyes of most Russians, therefore, after serving two terms as president, he felt comfortable passing the job off to his young assistant — Dmitry Medvedev.

But in the winter of 2011-12, massive public demonstrations in Moscow and St. Petersburg revealed that the nation's urban middle class — the university education privileged cosmopolitans — was disenchanted with his rule. They were joined by a small number of communists, nationalists, and other opponents of his Power Vertical. Staunch supporters who lived in the hinterland and occupied the lower rungs of the socio-economic ladder, the provincials, were also getting restive. Even some members of Putin's own team deserted him; for example, his former economic Czar, Alexei Kudrin, resigned rather than support the dramatic increase in the defense budget and was joined by some oligarchs and celebrities.

This medley of opponents accused Putin of rigging the 2011 Duma elections and his own re-election in 2012. To make matters worse, it was forecasted that Russia's hydrocarbon production would decline, while outmoded enterprises would prove incapable of surviving global competition. Henceforth, revenues would neither sustain social services nor an expanding defense budget, so both Putin's domestic and foreign policy agenda was in peril. It was only a matter of time before his reign expired along with the Power Vertical.

But soon after Putin began his third term, analysts claimed that predictions of his imminent demise were premature. In spite of a slippage in the polls, he remained the most popular politician in Russia, while his opponents were divided, demoralized, and leaderless. Measures he took to silence them—including restrictions on public demonstrations and the arrest of opposition leaders—convinced many middle class protestors that they had been too hasty in openly demanding his ouster. In an attempt to secure the provincials support, Putin exploited anti-Americanism sentiment that resonated among millions of Russians and portrayed his democratic detractors as agents of foreign governments.

On the international front, Putin has reasserted Russia's influence throughout the space of the former Soviet Union. He has done so with mixed results; for example, he has exploited Russia's energy assets to hamper Armenia and Ukraine in their Westward drive, but his alternative Economic Union has stalled.

As the United States reassesses relations with Russia and develops a strategic doctrine that addresses a turbulent international security environment, a brace of pivotal question remains to be answered: What is in store for Putin's future and for the fate of the Power Vertical? What do the answers to these questions mean for U.S.-Russian relations?

The purpose of this monograph is to address all of these questions and provide conclusions and recommendations to help U.S. policymakers provide appropriate answers to them. To accomplish this ambitious undertaking, two sets of scenarios will be considered. The first set is benign and include "The Status Quo" and "The Western Path to Development." The second set is malignant and includes what has been called, "Stalin Lite" and what amounts to a worst case scenario, "Russia in Chaos."

In looking at the first set of benign scenarios, the following observations are pertinent:

Status Quo: A broad range of economic and political circumstances support the notion that in spite of a multitude of challenges, the Power Vertical will persist even beyond Vladimir Putin's tenure. It is against this backdrop that a rebalance in U.S.-Russian relations will be evaluated.

The Western Path to Development: A faltering economy, pressure from progressives in the Kremlin, a revitalized "democracy movement," and disgruntled business oligarchs and grassroots upheaval in the provinces will ultimately produce a more open political system and law-based society. Under these circumstances, Russia's integration into the Euro-Atlantic community is plausible.

In addressing the second set of malignant scenarios, the following observations are pertinent:

Stalin Lite: In keeping with the crackdown that began soon after Putin was elected in 2012, a host of opposition figures were arrested, a number of oligarchs fled the country, new restraints were imposed upon the media and nongovernmental organizations, and members of the inner circle whose loyalty was suspect were removed from office. Under these circumstances, the prospects for a rebalance in U.S.-Russian relations are slim.

Russia in Chaos: Here, there is a collapse in the Power Vertical along with a dramatic economic decline, and Russia appears to be following the path of the former Soviet Union. This outcome may be less plausible than any of the above, but should it materialize, it will have significant and dangerous implications for international stability in general and U.S. international interests in particular. In sum, what happens next in Russia will have profound consequences for the security of the United States and its allies. Russia remains the largest country in the world; most of the earth's population and resources are found near it; and it is the only power that has the capacity to destroy the United States in a nuclear strike.

Russia must remain a U.S. major concern as American policymakers address two pivotal security challenges: a rebooting of the Euro-Atlantic security system that may ultimately include Russia, and an Asian Pivot that acknowledges that Russia is a major player in the Far East. While some analysts claim that clashing values necessitate a pause in relations, U.S.-Russian leaders must work toward a peaceful resolution of the crises in Syria, Iran, and North Korea.

The unexpected turbulent events of September 2013 that have resulted in a United Nations resolution compelling Syria to surrender its chemical weapons and restart in Geneva, Switzerland, to find a diplomatic resolution to the Syrian crisis offers evidence that a partnership, even if limited and fragile, is plausible. A major consideration of the U.S. national security establishment must be how to operationalize such a partnership.

For all intents and purposes, the United States and Russia now have taken responsibility for resolving the Syrian civil war and in the process have reached a new chapter in the reset of their relations. If they succeed in finding a diplomatic solution to the Syrian situation, further cooperation on other security matters will follow. If not, they will take a turn for the worse.

RUSSIA AFTER PUTIN

Note: This research was completed in the fall of 2013, which was obviously prior to the recent crisis in Crimea and Ukraine.

INTRODUCTION

In the winter of 2011-12, Russians expressed their outrage with Vladimir Putin in massive, unprecedented street protests. At one point, about 100,000 Muscovites braved the brutal cold and demanded his ouster and the demise of his system of rule known as the Power Vertical: a regime marked by personal rule and relationships.

> A small number of trusted figures around Mr. Putin, perhaps twenty to thirty people, make the key decisions. At the very top is an even tighter inner circle of about half a dozen individuals, all with close ties to Putin, who have worked together for twenty years, beginning in St. Petersburg and continuing in Moscow. Real decision making power resides inside the inner circle; while Russia's formal political institutions have to varying degrees been emasculated.[1]

One of the most prominent organizers, Alexey Navalny, a blogger of renown, stunned government officials when he proclaimed that the throng was large:

> enough . . . to seize the Kremlin and the White House now, but we won't as we are peaceful people, but sooner or later we will take back what is rightfully ours.[2]

Similar displays of public anger, albeit in smaller numbers, erupted in St. Petersburg and other cities and via TV and the Internet, mesmerized a global audience of billions. Even hard-edged pundits pondered whether they were witnessing a Russian version of the Arab Spring and the forced exit of autocratic rulers. Cowed by Czars and Soviet dictators for centuries, Russians were now about to cast out their tormentors.

This historic outburst had its roots in the September 2011 announcement that Putin would run for a third term as president and not Dmitry Medvedev, who was an open advocate of government transparency and pluralism. Putin's proclamation abruptly demonstrated that Medvedev was a mere puppet responding to the tugs of his master. More bad news arrived that December when it was revealed that the parliamentary elections had been rigged. This was in keeping with Putin's penchant for "overkill" since his United Russia would have swept the field even if the elections were fair, but when his personal power was at risk, he did not take chances.

The demonstrations uplifted the spirits of the Russians who yearned to live in a truly democratic society, and many of the protesters concluded that they did not need Medvedev to accomplish that cherished objective. They could achieve it through bottom-up reform. Putin's newly assertive opposition consisted of a medley of individuals and interests. Those most visible included middle class urbanites, cosmopolitans who had college degrees, ate sushi, and took foreign vacations—the very people Putin needed to restore the state, to diversify the economy and to transform Russia into a modern society. Clearly, this generation was not spooked by the same show of force that had intimidated their parents. They were not afraid! They were joined in smaller numbers by a motley crew of communists and nationalists that included some of the most prominent new and assertive leaders like Navalny, who gained national notoriety via his blog and campaigns to fight corruption, and Sergei Udaltsov, a leftist provocateur who proclaimed that he and his supporters favored the immediate ouster of Putin and his ilk. The bold behavior of these two men indicated that something truly significant was abroad in Russia.[3]

Sharing platforms with these two firebrands were liberals with familiar names like Boris Nemstov and Gregory Yavlinsky, both of whom had served in past governments. But in addition to these "old-timers" and disgruntled middle class protesters, members of Putin's team like Alexei Kudrin—a former finance minister—joined them in a turbulent protest on Moscow's Sakharov Square. He had parted with Putin over a decision to sustain a bloated defense budget at the expense of other public programs. He was accompanied by former Putin staffers and one time admirers, for example, Kseniya Sobchak, a huge TV celebrity and daughter of Putin's old boss, Anatoly Sobchak, a one-time St. Petersburg Mayor. Obviously ignoring the fate of the imprisoned Mikhail Khodorkovsky, some of the country's richest men, for example, Mikhail Prochorov, joined the protestors. Some pundits believed that like leaders of the "opposition" parties in the Duma, he was a Kremlin stooge, a stage-prop Putin could cite to burnish his democratic credentials. That said, the cosmopolitan activists were receiving economic aid from some oligarchs—people who had learned how to cover their backside or who believed that change was inevitable.

Although demonstrations in Moscow and St. Petersburg captured the attention of the international media, Putin remained the county's most popular politician. His stock, however, was in decline even among loyal followers in the vast Russian hinterland. Unlike the cosmopolitans, these people, the provincials, did not enjoy much formal education, fancy foreign culinary treats, nor vacations abroad. At the same time, they abhorred Western values and resented being lectured by Russia's critics. On the contrary, they were outspoken anti-Americans who remained tethered to old Soviet enterprises or were retirees living in the desolate hinterland surviving on government entitlements. For them, Putin was the iconic strongman that their ancestors celebrated throughout history — a tough protector of Mother Russia. At the same time, he could take credit for a vast improvement in conditions for tens of millions of Russians. Consequently, they had given him their unqualified support during his first two terms as president. By 2012, many now associated his rule with economic inequality, corruption, lawlessness, and little or no improvement in public services. But, as of yet, they were not prepared to openly support Putin's opponents.

While the road ahead was shrouded in mist, Kremlin-watchers predicted a sea change in Russian politics. Many doubted that Putin would survive his third term, and their analysis rested largely upon the expectation that he would be upended by the same economic pitfalls that toppled his Soviet predecessors: most specifically, a decline in gas and oil output, deflated prices for those commodities, and the failure of the Kremlin to provide the country with a Plan B. That is the failure to diversify a one-legged petro economy and to create economic activity in a variety of areas that allowed Russia to compete in the brutal global market. As gas and oil revenues plunged, Putin could no longer meet the promises that he made to his base — the provincials — and provide them with jobs, pensions, and social welfare services, while meeting the demands of the military-industrial complex. He promised the generals and present-day replicas of the Red Managers a spike in the defense budget even though they wanted to maintain large and expensive general purpose forces — presumably to match American military power — that clear-headed defense analysts deemed irrational and dangerous.

Calls for his removal were sustained by pandemic corruption and other forms of lawless behavior and growing resentment that a handful of oligarchs and members of pro-Putin clans were living in luxury while the average Russian was struggling to make ends meet. In addition to surging popular disgruntlement, there were signs of discontent among Putin's associates who relied upon his protection but were worried about their economic welfare. Like their Soviet counterparts a generation ago, they could not ignore the alarming observation that privileged members of society — including "their kids" — were among the demonstrators. Many younger members of the ruling elite believed there was trouble ahead if the problems that had ignited unprecedented protest were ignored. Some concluded that it was prudent to join the future rulers that were emerging from the gathering storm and not oppose them.

But there was a two-fold problem with this prognosis. First, the demonstrators soon left the streets, many even before Putin launched a crackdown on public protests, and accused their leaders of criminal behavior. They were not only divided by culture and ideology, they had no single leader to rally them, nor did they have a viable political program or any firm idea about how they were going to press forward in an organized fashion. Then Putin passed a medley of laws that portrayed any recipient of assistance from abroad a "foreign agent," expelled the U.S. Information Agency (USIA) for peddling subversion in Russia, redefined the meaning of traitorous behavior, and took other measures to silence the pesky protestors. By the end of the year, foreign journalists reported that many of the younger members of the middle class got the message and, like their parents, "They, too, are afraid."

A second problem was that those who predicted the Power Vertical's demise found themselves tongue-tied when asked a pertinent question: "What would replace it?" In the words of several highly respected Russian analysts, "That Russia is in crisis is becoming apparent. What are less apparent are the exact nature and the stakes and options involved."[4]

This monograph is an attempt to answer the question: "After Putin and the Power Vertical, what next?" Given the prevailing inattention to the "Russian Question" among the American foreign policy community, Russia's fate has been treated as a sideshow in Washington. There has been some discussion in the White House about the prospects for a "re-balance" in American-Russian relations that would address issues that concern both countries, but the Congress, the media, and the public has shown little interest in the enterprise. For most Americans, what happens in Russia is of little consequence and for members of Congress and the national security community, the most compelling challenges are unfolding in Asia. In addition to the reckless comments and threatening behavior of the nuclear-armed leadership in North Korea, China has been throwing its weight around in much of Asia, prompting many analysts to see trouble ahead with Beijing.

To minimize the Russian Question is unwarranted and could be dangerous. Only Russia can destroy the United States in a nuclear strike, holds a valued veto at the United Nations (UN) and covers a vast area of the world where much of the earth's population and resources can be found. Furthermore, a truculent uncooperative Russia may obstruct U.S. foreign policy priorities. What happens next in Russia, then, is of great consequence for the global security environment and therefore of paramount concern to the United States.

Toward this end, two sets of scenarios resting on a medley of analysis, facts, trends and projections will be assessed as far as the mid-2020s. The first set is benign and includes "The Status Quo" and a "Western Path to Development." The second set is malignant and includes what has been called, "Stalin Lite," i.e., a return to a limited police state at home and revisionism abroad. It also includes what amounts to a worst case scenario, "Russia in Chaos," where central authority is weak, the economy is dysfunctional, violence widespread, and de facto fiefdoms based on ethnic, ideological, regional, and religious divisions proliferate. Under these turbulent and unpredictable circumstances, all of Eurasia is at risk but the primary focus will be upon American-Russian relations.

In looking at the set of benign outcomes, the following observations are pertinent.

The Status Quo: In spite of a multitude of challenges — economic, political and social — the Power Vertical prevails with or without Vladimir Putin's stewardship. The relationship between the West and Russia remains problematic, although there are notably areas of cooperation.

The Western Path to Development: Under mounting pressure from progressive members of his team and business oligarchs, as well as a revitalized "democracy movement" and discontent among the provincials, Putin reluctantly retreats and paves the way for a more open political system and law-based society. Prospects for close relations with the West improve dramatically and make possible the integration of an enlarged Europe, including Russia.

In addressing the second set of malignant scenarios, the following observations are pertinent.

Stalin Lite: In keeping with the crackdown that began soon after Putin was elected in 2012, a host of opposition figures are arrested, a number of oligarchs flee the country, new restraints are imposed upon the media, nongovernmental organizations (NGOs), and members of the inner circle whose loyalty is suspect are removed from office. Intercommunal violence is on the rise throughout Russia, not only in the North Caucasus. Simultaneously, under the influence of Slavic ultra-nationalists, the Kremlin lashes out at Azerbaijan, the Baltics, Georgia, and Ukraine. "East-West relations" take on the aspects of a "new cold war," but the Kremlin overlords acknowledge that the correlation of forces favors the West, and it is foolhardy to risk a military confrontation with the North Atlantic Treaty Organization (NATO) or its member states. In short, they adhere to "red lines" that they will not cross.

Russia in Chaos: A multitude of rival factions divide the Kremlin overlords, while disparate ethnic, religious and regional actors dominate a host of fiefdoms that challenge Moscow's authority. Meanwhile, the military and police have become dysfunctional and their members demoralized. In some cases, they have joined the disparate armed groups that are responsible for widespread violence. Under these circumstances, Russia may fragment in much the same fashion that the Union of Soviet Socialist Republics (USSR) did.

Russian-watchers deem this outcome implausible but should it materialize, it will have monumental and dangerous implications for international stability and force U.S. strategists to take another look at Russia. In contrast to the Stalin Lite scenario, the major players — out of design or happenstance — are prepared to take risks and actions that may foster violent conflicts with Russia's neighbors and Western allies in the former Soviet space.

Each of the scenarios will be considered to determine their impact upon Russia and the countries that are adjacent to it in Eurasia — although the major focus will be upon Europe. The implications for U.S.-Russian relations will receive special attention in each of the four scenarios.

Pertinent questions that need to be answered include the following:

- Why will Russia continue to be a major concern of the American foreign policy community?
- What are the prospects for fruitful cooperation between the United States and Russia on a range of critical international problems?
- What issues at present are most favorable to cooperation between the two countries?
- Why, since 2007, has Putin concluded that the United States can no longer dictate to Russia but must treat it like an equal, and what impact will his crackdown have upon the prospects for fruitful cooperation with the Barack Obama administration?
- What are the domestic U.S. barriers to a re-engagement with Russia?
- In looking at the four scenarios under scrutiny, what are their significance for stability in Europe and harmonious American-Russian relations?

- How does China influence the prospects for positive American-Russian relations?
- Why must the United States seek a partnership with Russia on addressing crises like Syria, Iran and North Korea and not embrace a pause in relations as some analysts recommend?

THE STATUS QUO

The Domestic Prospect.

By the close of 2012, analysts predicting Putin's demise were having second thoughts. His popularity was slumping, but he still enjoyed a 60 percent favorability rating in the polls. Democratic leaders everywhere would characterize such staunch support as a "ruling mandate." The principle reason for this reassessment was that in face of his crackdown, most protestors returned to the comfort of their homes. Wags in Moscow proclaimed, "They forgot about revolution and went shopping!"

There was much about Putin's meteoric rise that baffled Kremlin-watchers. He was born and educated in Leningrad and, after graduating with a law degree, he entered the KGB. He served for 4 years in the East German city of Dresden where, according to his biographers, one of his major duties was to monitor the activities of those German comrades who clashed with Eric Honecker, the reactionary leader who earned Moscow's enmity for resisting the liberal reforms that Gorbachev had championed in the USSR and urged Moscow's satellites to follow. Was Putin working with the dissidents in a Kremlin orchestrated plot to dump Honecker? If so, he might have been a much more substantial member of the KGB than his resume otherwise indicated.

In 1990 he returned to his hometown, and in 3 years, he hopscotched from being an aide to St. Petersburg's Mayor Sobchak, his former law professor, to much bigger things in Moscow. After Sobchak had lost his bid for re-election, Putin went to work in the President's office; was appointed head of the FSB (the new name for the KGB); became deputy prime minister; and served as acting prime minister before he replaced Yeltsin as president.

It appears that Putin, while in St. Petersburg, had developed the capacity to serve as an interlocutor between the government and the new business oligarchs that had become powerful players in political as well as economic affairs in the midst of post-Soviet turmoil. Presumably, one of the reasons why he was selected to replace Yeltsin was to make sure that the oligarchs did not break the arrangement that the Kremlin had made with them: "Take whatever you could get your hands on in the economic realm but do not meddle in the political realm."[5]

After his third successful run for the presidency, Putin adopted new laws and procedures that intimidated his opponents—curtailing public protests by making it more difficult to conduct them legally, by denying NGO activists access to foreign funding, by redefining the word "traitorous," and by censoring bloggers, to name several of them. Even the toothless Duma attracted his attention; for example, Gennadi V. Gudkov, a rare member of the parliament who challenged the government, was removed from office on the ground that he had engaged in "criminal behavior."[6]

In March, the residencies of Navalny, Sobchak, and several other protest leaders were stormed and their contents rifled. Criminal charges were leveled against Navalny and the leftist fire-brand Sergei Udaltsov, clearly a prologue for worse things to come. Furthermore, one of the latter's associates, Leonid Razvozzhayev, who fled to Kiev to avoid arrest, was kidnapped and returned to a Russian prison. He had arranged a transit to Israel with a Jewish agency but, while taking a break in his meeting with its representatives, he was snatched by Russian agents and taken home where he was accused of visa irregularities.

Shaken by the crackdown, most protestors vacated the streets and resorted to less provocative enterprises, while their titular leaders vainly searched for a new strategy. Like the architects of the Arab Spring, they turned to the Internet and formed a Coordinating Council of 45 activists. Navalny, who had gained notoriety by claiming Putin's United Russia was "the party of thieves and crooks," was chosen its leader. It included representatives from all factions, although the cosmopolitans predominated. Their purpose was to remove Putin from power but, when asked how they intended to accomplish that daunting objective, their answers were vague.

Nonetheless many foreign observers were sanguine about their prospects. After all, the Arab Spring had demonstrated the capacity of grassroots protesters to shape political events with the help of the new information technology that was available to ordinary citizens. Putin controlled the media, but because he did not use computers and dismissed the power of cell phones and social networking, he was operating in the dark surrounded by "yes men." Granted it would take time, but the handwriting was on the wall; the days of the Power Vertical were numbered.[7]

Some Russian commentators were less optimistic, citing overwhelming evidence that the reformers had failed to live up to expectations. Navalny was characterized as a windbag whose nationalistic affiliations unsettled the democrats; the Council was denigrated as a Potemkin-like fraud; and there was ample evidence that the reformers were demoralized. Meanwhile, Putin continued his crackdown and, while it did not silence the likes of Navalny and Udaltsov, it intimidated ordinary disgruntled members of the urban middle class. They had little stomach for a confrontation with Putin's security services. Holding well-paying jobs and having access to the good life that had been denied their parents, not many of them were prepared to take risks. Yes, they were unhappy with the government, but if the average Russian did not butt heads with the authorities, they left you alone and your private affairs were your own business. What other Russian generation could make a similar statement?

Putin's harsh policies were accompanied by a populist campaign as he appeared before audiences of workers to commiserate with them. He even met with members of motorcycle gangs that celebrated Russian chauvinism and vehemently attacked non-Russians. They did so with special zeal in the case of Muslims. Moreover, while sophisticated Muscovites lamented the jail sentence for two young women who belonged to the Pussy Riot rock group that had conducted a bizarre display of contempt for Putin in Moscow's Church of the Redeemer, most ordinary folk applauded the punishment.

Putin displayed a unique gift for exploiting the wide cultural chasm that separated the cosmopolitans and the provincials through his populist rhetoric and widely circulated visuals: his stalking wild animals, searching for archeological treasure in ocean depths, and flying in flimsy aircraft guiding migratory birds to a safe refuge. He often performed these feats shirt-less or in macho sports togs. Critics made fun of such displays, but Putin knew that "simple" folk liked it when their leaders acted and talked tough. Millions of Russians still recalled with approval his threat to kill Chechen terrorists in their outdoor "shit-houses."

They also were delighted by his attacks on Ameri-can officials interfering in Russia's domestic affairs. Days after arriving in Moscow, the new American Ambassador, Michael McFaul—a Stanford Univer-sity professor and one of the major proponents of the reset—was stalked by a TV crew, sending a message from the Kremlin that his mission in Moscow was not going to be pleasant. Also, Putin named Secretary of State Hillary Clinton a "foreign provocateur" bent on achieving regime change in Russia. Such claims reso-nated among ordinary folk and so did accusations that the reformers were nothing less than "foreign agents" who were seeking the government's overthrow. Even some Russians who scoffed at such tactics were dis-turbed by what they deemed American efforts to hu-miliate Russia. In his public appearances, Putin often reminded onlookers that the Americans were not in a position to preach to anyone. How could they do so when the 2000 presidential election was stolen; or demonize Russia for corruption when the global fi-nancial crisis orchestrated by Wall Street represented the most massive act of corruption ever? And human rights—well, every day the evidence was overwhelm-ing that the Americans in their endless wars were the major perpetrators of such abhorrent practices, and what about the U.S. prison population—said to be the largest in the world?

By year's end, Kremlin-watchers concluded that predictions of Putin's imminent political demise were baseless. On the contrary, not only would he survive until 2018, his health willing, he might ride a third term into the 2020s. Yes, there were many reasons for complaints, but no one could deny Russians were living better than ever, could travel abroad, and they did not have to worry about clumsy government intrusions into their daily lives. Putin gave them a psychological jolt by once again making them proud of their country. In sum, since Putin was in charge, things had changed for the better. All one had to do was reflect on recent history.

In the aftermath of the USSR's disintegration, "Russia's gross domestic product [GDP] contracted by as much as 35-45 percent."[8] In contrast to the Soviet Union's last year, living standards collapsed by 46 percent and, after its demise, Russia was stricken by a budget deficit and a ruble devaluation that devastated personal wealth. It was no surprise, then, that voters expressed little enthusiasm for Boris Yeltsin, who eagerly embraced foreign inspired economic bromides — e.g., the "shock therapy" that was associated with American free market radicals. The aging and sickly Yeltsin's incompetence was compounded by his complicity in the "great robbery" that he tolerated — nay participated in — with a small group of grasping oligarchs. It resulted in a colossal heist of national wealth, pandemic corruption, and economic hard times for just about everybody except the new Nomenklatura.

"Then, as if by magic, everything seemed to begin changing in 1999."[9] Henceforth the nation's GDP grew by an annual rate of 7 percent, incomes soared for many, the budget deficit plunged, and Russia settled its foreign debt obligations. On the political front, Putin, who was named Prime Minister, was unabashed in his pledge to the Russian people that he would end their long, dark period of humiliation. Toward that end, he launched a second war in Chechnya and crushed the "bandits" there and adopted tough new measures to silence troublemakers, including the most "assertive" oligarchs. The incarceration of Lukoil's president, Mikhail Khodorkovsky, earned Putin enmity outside of Russia but applause within it. In Putin's mind, and that of a majority of Russians, there was a direct correlation between stability—authoritarianism—and prosperity. "Russia was back!"

Nonetheless, upon his 2012 return to the Presidential Palace, Putin had reason to look toward a third term with trepidation. He agreed that his Achilles heel was the "petro-state" where an entire nation rested on a one-legged economy. He, too, endorsed the notion of economic diversification but that entailed a real war on corruption, a truly functional legal system, and other liberal measures that threaten the privileges of his most powerful supporters. That meant taking on the muscular collection of former security officers, military commanders, economic warlords, and criminal elements that embraced the status quo. It had made them rich and influential, and they saw no reason to scrap it.

At the same time, abundant gas and oil profits in the early-21st century were barriers to change just as they were during the Soviet era. In the last years of its existence, the Soviet Union's hydrocarbon revenues surged, and this windfall allowed the geriatric leadership to avoid one of the specters that haunted most of them: the Soviet system's implosion. Convinced that oil and gas revenues would continue to flow, changes in either the economic or political system were unnecessary. There was a sufficient supply of rubles to fund both the Warfare and Welfare State, or so they reasoned, until hydrocarbon production faltered and Mikhail Gorbachev was forced to acknowledge that the USSR could not afford both "guns and butter."

This all deteriorated during Yeltsin's 10 years in the Kremlin, but soon after Putin was appointed prime minister, he counted on high energy prices to keep the generals happy and through government transfers to meet the needs of ordinary folk. Furthermore, Russia's economic boom opened avenues of prosperity to an expanding educated middle class. Life improved as well for millions of other Russians who did not enjoy much formal education as they found jobs in construction, service industries, and other occupations not directly tied to the energy boom. As the hard times of the Yeltsin era were left behind them, the people embraced the "Putin era."[10]

But he hit a bump when the economic crisis of 2008 demonstrated how vulnerable Russia remained in the face of dramatic changes in the global economy. Alexei Kudrin, who served as finance minister from 2000 to 2011, observed that Russia's problems were a direct result of its dependence upon hydrocarbon rents. "The oil industry" no longer was "a locomotive for the economy" but had "become a brake." This had been the fate of any country that depended upon a single commodity for prosperity. At the same time, economists predicted the output of energy assets would decline after 2020.[11] If Russia was to become a modern society capable of competing in the global economy, it had to find wealth-producing opportunities other than living on rents derived from natural resources. That meant resurrecting industry, expanding the service sector, and investing in roads, air fields, and a multitude of other infrastructure improvements. In his public remarks, Putin spoke in favor of diversification, but he was reluctant to take the measures necessary to accomplish that daunting objective. On the contrary, his actions seemed to be in keeping with those in the military-industrial complex that saw massive defense spending as a force multiplier for the economy. Putin was by far the most powerful man in Russia, but he could not altogether ignore the disparate clans that had the capacity to challenge him.

Analysts focusing on declining gas and oil rents, however, had ignored a more positive picture: Russia still had abundant hydrocarbon wealth, and the older energy fields were profitable if new techniques were adopted. The large Western oil companies were ready to provide the capital required to modernize the depleted wells in western Siberia. What is more, access to oil and gas fields in the Arctic were so attractive that foreign entrepreneurs would gladly invest in them as well.

Kremlin officials believed that prices would firm up as the global economy rebounded in 2013. In a pinch, Putin could rely upon his ace in the hole: the world's third largest stockpile of hard currency. Should hydrocarbon revenues stall, Putin presumed that he had the cash to meet the complaints of those in the hinterland who expressed fears about their salaries and pensions. Many remained silent because they accepted the Kremlin line that "Yes, we are facing hard times but so are the Europeans who not only are struggling to save the Euro but to salvage the EU [European Union] itself." Then, too, Russians throughout history had demonstrated they had a higher tolerance for pain than their spoiled fellow Europeans. Consequently, Greeks and Spaniards might be more inclined to press for regime change than ordinary Russians. Even the arrogant

Americans were having trouble addressing their gargantuan debt crisis and economic inequality there was unprecedented. The U.S. media was percolating with reports that the "American Dream" was beyond the grasp of a growing number of U.S. citizens.

In Russia, by contrast, economic diversification was taking place. One of Russia's unheralded economic assets included a large pool of almost 150 million customers who craved the living standards of a consumer economy that had long flourished in Europe and the United States. Foreign investors were more than happy to invest in an authoritarian "European" country just as they had done so for decades in the world's most populated Asian autocracy—China. At the same time, there were some positive signs on the demographic front; deaths still exceeded births, but migrants from many parts of the former USSR were entering Russia in steady numbers. It was reported that most of the workers building the Sochi Olympic venue were from Central Asia. If this trend was sustained, it was good news for both Russia and those who courted its consumers.

What's more, Russia could claim with justification that it was on the road to diversification as rents from oil and gas capitalized jobs in industry, construction, and the service sector. Reports from Nizhny Novgorod indicated in late-2012 that GM would invest over $1 billion in upgrading Russian auto plants. Foreign car sales were increasing at a rapid pace, and it was projected that Russia would surpass Germany as Europe's largest car market. GM and other foreign automakers were also establishing joint ventures with Russian manufacturers such as Avtovaz. While economists focused on China and India as the leading BRIC

(Brazil, Russia, India, and China) countries when it came to cars, Russia was in the lead.

> There are now 250 cars for every 1,000 people in Russia, which places the country about midway between emerging markets in Asia and developed markets in Europe. By comparison, India has 11 cars for every 1,000 people; China 49, . . ."[12]

Of course, there were frequent expressions of discontent with the Power Vertical from the hinterland; corruption along with pervasive lawlessness in business was one of the most serious threats to Putin and his camp. But as long as there was sufficient revenue to meet their basic needs, the provincials would not take to the streets in large numbers. Simultaneously, by granting the local economic and political elites some concessions — such as a greater voice in matters that affected their regions and a modest uptick in revenues from Moscow — they would not transform their harsh rhetoric and threats to bolt from the federation into resolute action.

"Bandits" continued to wage a low-level insurgency in the North Caucasus, but efforts on the part of foreign jihadists to exploit Islamic discontent in Russia had only achieved marginal results. Fears about Muslims and other minorities supporting independence movements had not materialized to any significant degree as the ethnic minority leadership calculated that the risks of leaving Russia were greater than the rewards of remaining within its boundaries. At the same time, the disparate Islamic factions were at odds with each other much as Sunni and Shiite were in other parts of the Umma and nationalistic rivalry was added to the mix.

The International Prospect.

In 2007, Putin reversed a course of cooperation with President George W. Bush when at the annual security affairs conference in Munich, Germany, he announced the end of the American unipolar moment; henceforth his partner in Washington had to treat him as an equal—not a supplicant—if Bush hoped to work with him. By this time, Putin was not optimistic because he concluded that while Russia made a number of concessions in the area of nuclear arms control, Bush responded by scrapping the Cold War anti-ballistic missile (ABM) treaty and by proclaiming plans for an anti-missile system in Europe. For Putin, that was it; henceforth, he would only engage with his counterparts in Washington if they gave him something in return for his concessions. He also acted as if the Americans needed him more then he needed them.

Analysts in Washington retorted that by any measuring stick, Russia was not a military equal to the United States, and Putin's international ambitions were out of sync with his nation's capabilities. Yes, it had a nuclear arsenal only second to the United States, a veto at the UN, and controlled massive territory to shape global affairs. Consequently, it could make life difficult for the West as it had in the case of Syria, but in any assessment of the "correlation of forces" between the United States and Russia, all one had to do was to Google "population," "GDP," and other data that compared the two, and the United States enjoyed an enormous advantage in shaping world affairs. Add the population, GDP, and other measures of power of Washington's allies in Europe and Asia, and the "West's" advantage was even more gargantuan. In a word, such musings indicated why Russia was of little interest to most members of Congress and their constituents. What really concerned them was the looming presence of China, not another failed European empire.

Looking at Russia's foreign policy priorities from Putin's perspective, however, one can reach a conclusion more favorable to him. He knows Russia will never enjoy the power that the Soviet leaders did, and this may explain why he gave Medvedev the American and European portfolios. He has no intention of taking on the West in a serious showdown because his most urgent foreign policy goal is regional, not international—although the region in question, the former Soviet space, is massive. Specifically, he wants to re-integrate former Soviet entities back into Russia's clutches and to deny the West the capacity to integrate them into the EU and NATO. Using this measuring stick, Putin's foreign policy agenda shows promise as many analysts in Eastern Europe remind their American counterparts.

Belarus, Kazakhstan, and Ukraine, the countries of most immediate concern to the foreign ministry, may challenge Putin at times, but in the final analysis, he has significant influence over all three of them. While Belarus and Kazakhstan are deemed important to Moscow, control over Ukraine is a must for Russia. Without control of Ukraine, any effort on Russia's part to throw its weight around in Eurasia is placed in peril. Ukraine no longer expresses interest in NATO, although Moscow is not happy about its attraction to the EU. Russian analysts, of course, have reason to conclude that just as infighting among the democrats in Ukraine paved the way for the election of a pro-Russian president, Viktor Yanukovych, those in control of Kiev today will fail in their bid for EU membership as a consequence of their own ineptitude and political ambitions.

Simultaneously, Georgia remains committed to NATO membership but since the Five-Day War, the major European powers, and the United States as well, have retreated from a campaign to find a place for it in the alliance. It is with this observation in mind, that the Russians can claim that, while foreign observers have dwelt upon their army's difficulties and shortfalls in waging the 2008 war, in the final analysis, they won it.

Officials in the Russian foreign ministry also can take comfort in the fact that they dominate the Trans-Dniester and Armenia and have significant influence in Moldova. What is more, through its powerful business interests, Russia has the means to influence the cultural, economic and political affairs of Estonia, Latvia, and Lithuania, and some East European countries that were former Soviet satellites.

In short, throughout the 1990s and early-2000s Moscow devoted much of its foreign policy energy and funds to transforming its former Soviet empire into a sphere of influence.[13]

Once many of the targeted countries gained EU and NATO membership, this campaign fell short, but Russian interests play an important part in their politics, economy, and media. Ambitious young businessmen in Eastern Europe are once again finding it useful to speak Russian and profitable to court Russian companies that control banks, media outlets, and most energy enterprises. The political elite in all of these countries cannot be unmindful of their large neighbor to the east, especially as the EU wrestles with persistent economic problems and Euro-Skeptics gain electoral support among their disgruntled populations.

Former Soviet entities that now belong to the EU can rely upon its assistance, but the EU is not always forthcoming. For years, powerful business interests—especially but not exclusively in Germany—resented the ability of the new members to influence profitable deals with Russia; as yet, the EU has failed to develop a truly comprehensive energy security policy to protect them from the power of Gazprom; Brussels, Belgium also has turned its back on Moscow's capacity to influence internal economic and political affairs through deals that local entrepreneurs "cannot afford to refuse." Today, preoccupation with the debt and Euro crisis has compelled some EU members to placate the Russians on their own, and logic dictates that in the process they must make concessions favorable to what in Soviet days they called their "elder brother."[14]

In looking toward Putin's foreign policy priorities, he is pursuing several important interrelated goals:

- Deny former Soviet Republics in the near abroad the opportunity to follow the Baltic Republics into NATO and the EU; Belarus, Georgia, and Ukraine in particular.
- Instead, incorporate them, as well as the Central Asia states, into economic and security systems dominated by Moscow—e.g., Collective Security Treaty Organization (CSTO) and a new Eurasian Economic Union.
- Join China in a grand strategy to present the Americans with a firewall in every part of Eurasia, and do the same in denying Washington successful attempts to achieve regime change throughout Eurasia and the Greater Middle East. Of course, Moscow will avoid any effort on Beijing's part to treat Russia like a junior partner.

- Cooperate with the West in some areas of common concern: nuclear proliferation, Islamic terrorism, and other threats to both camps. But in contrast to Yeltsin, Putin will demand compensation in return: e.g., have a voice in the American anti-missile system in Europe and provide Russia with a voice in efforts to address the crises in Iran and Syria. With Pakistan on the verge of civil war, the Americans may lean more heavily upon the Northern Distribution Network in their exit from Afghanistan than the perilous southern route through Pakistan.[15]

This scenario is the "most plausible" since it represents current circumstances and may endure even if Putin is no longer in charge. Some may question using the word "benign" to describe it since Putin is doing things deserving of a more negative connotation. But in defense of this designation, civil society is alive in Russia, although under assault. There are independent newspapers, and radio and TV outlets that consistently criticize Putin and his associates. And, of course, there is the Internet that not only reaches the educated through English language material but increasingly in Russian. The Kremlin has taken steps to neutralize it, but it continues to flourish. From time to time, the Kremlin and Putin's policies are subjectively scrutinized by media that is under the control of the ruling class.

The status quo may persist essentially unchanged for years but there are signs that it may presage the second most likely outcome: Stalin Lite that is deserving of the "malignant" designation. But before looking at it, what about the other "benign" scenario, that is, The Western Path to Development? It will be discussed next.

THE WESTERN PATH TO DEVELOPMENT

The Domestic Prospect.

This outcome rests upon the conventional wisdom among Kremlin-watchers that the collapse of Russia's "one-legged" petro-economy and a surge in grass-roots opposition to the Power Vertical are preconditions for Russia adopting a Western path to development—a free market economy, democratic polity, and pluralistic social system. Consider, therefore, the following train of events.

As a result of technological breakthroughs, the United States surges ahead of Russia as the world's leading exporter of natural gas and sells it for a price Gazprom cannot match. At the same time, by harvesting its enormous sand tar deposits, Canada provides petroleum on the global market at prices that Russian oil companies cannot match. In sum, North America's energy windfall undercuts the financial base of the hardliners in the Kremlin and opens the door for those who advocate a Western path to Russia's development.

During much of Putin's reign, Gazprom, the country's largest business enterprise accounted for almost 10 percent of Russia's GDP, 500,000 jobs, and 20 percent of the state's budget. But in the last quarter of 2012, its profits plunged 50 percent as "customers slashed orders and negotiated price discounts (China, for one) worth $4 billion in 2012 alone. . . . "[16] Under these circumstances, the company and the Russian government lost the capacity to dictate terms to its customers and neighboring governments. Oil rents also declined, and that trend had a profound impact upon Russia's budget since profits depended upon selling a barrel for about $115. Unfortunately, the world market settled upon a price far lower than that figure.

There was additional bad news for the reactionaries that depended upon energy wealth to dominate Russia: the long-expected drive to diversify the economy stalled as many investors—domestic and foreign—concluded that Russia remained a corrupt, lawless, dysfunctional society. Money could be made there but only at grave risk as many foreign firms adhered to rules that their Kremlin-connected Russian counterparts brazenly ignored. Among the oligarchs and their confederates, profits from energy represented easy pickings, while a truly energetic drive toward economic diversification would involve real entrepreneurial skills and uncertain profits. Even more unsettling, the subsequent shift in commerce would create new centers of influence that the oligarchs could not control; naturally, they balked at diversification for this reason alone.

Putin spoke incessantly about finding new areas of economic activity, lest Russia end up like other "petro-states" that ultimately faced economic doom when their gas and oil revenues slumped. But facts on the ground did not support his rhetoric. Russia's failure to diversify was exemplified by the following observation:

> Rapacious officeholders have reinforced the country's dependence on the oil industry by strangling independent enterprise. Small businesses employing fewer than 100 people make up less than 7 percent of Russia's economy as compared with Poland, for example, where they make up fully 50 percent.[17]

By design or happenstance, giant enterprises absorbed smaller firms and reduced, not enlarged, the number of businesses in Russia.

As a larger number of Russians from all walks of life became victims of economic decline, displays of political unrest surged and gave rise to new alliances that did not escape the attention of the more clear-headed in the government and associated clans. With revenues in a free-fall, the Kremlin found it exceedingly difficult to subsidize jobs and entitlements, and efforts to fight corruption took a back seat to the power elite's survival. This fed widespread expressions of discontent at the grassroots — including the hinterland where Putin had always been popular — and gave regional elites a political base among the disgruntled provincials. For years, regional stakeholders had pressed Moscow for a larger share of revenues and a greater voice in their own political affairs, but to no avail. Simultaneously, their constituents relied upon the federal government for their economic security. But as the center proved unwilling or incapable of providing jobs and safety nets to protect Russia's most vulnerable citizens, working people looked toward provincial elites for protection.

In Siberia, voices demanding outright breaks with the rest of Russia became more resonant. The federal bureaucrats, thousands of miles away, exploited wealth extracted from Siberian land, but its residents received crumbs in return. Local economic and political elites henceforth struck deals with their Asian neighbors and, in the process, found economic alternatives to Moscow. As a consequence, they kept much of the wealth that was produced in Russia's Far East. Elsewhere, minority communities acted in a similar fashion and ethnic communal pride served as a force multiplier in clashes with their "Russian masters." The jihadists in the North Caucasus attracted new recruits, and in many places they enjoyed de facto, if not de jure, independence. Here was further evidence that the hardliners in the Kremlin were incapable of keeping Russia whole.

The task of providing the military with funds to procure new weapon systems and to improve the quality of life for the troops and their families became even more daunting. Despite shrinking numbers, it became difficult to arm and train the troops; consequently, morale among enlisted men and officers plunged, causing grave concern about their loyalty. Defense tycoons objected to cuts in the military budget, and their disgruntled workers frequently did so through violent protest — occupying factories, blocking bridges and tunnels and halting auto and train traffic.

In addition to the revival of massive street demonstrations, the democrats were busy building a new movement that favored a Western, pluralistic world view. The 2011-12 demonstrations represented the "tip of the iceberg," but below it loomed a gathering force of grassroots power. Even after the cosmopolitans spurned massive street protests, they continued to organize and expand civil society through the Internet. Working in the most promising sectors of the economy, a growing legion of Russians — including young people who attended school, worked, and vacationed in Europe and the United States — was creating a counterculture and a narrative that aped the values and worldview integral to Western pluralism.

NGOs that provided the underpinning for volunteerism swept the country. Attempts to deny them foreign funding had a minimal impact upon their operations as they turned to domestic alternatives to expand a social network of like-minded people. While the State was moving toward the autocratic right, the most consequential members of society were lurching toward the democratic left. As one Russian Internet portal manager noted, ". . . formations of a new sort are being created within" the larger civil society. As the Arab Spring demonstrated, the Internet made it possible for democracy to flourish even in societies that were not democratic. The government controlled TV and adhered to an information strategy that rested upon the old Soviet formula of deceit, deception, and disinformation, but through the Web and "smart phones" millions of Russians had access to the truth and, in turn, through social networking passed it onto friends, neighbors, and other Web users. The Internet was a game changer upon which the Russian democrats were banking to lead their country down the road to an open, law-based society. It was estimated that by 2014 close to 70 percent of the country's adults would have Internet access. What is more, "Russia's largest Internet portals" had "already caught up with several federal television channels" in terms of users. The Kremlin, therefore, conceded that the Internet had become the major instrument of citizen "self-organization."[18] As a consequence, there was a spike in the arrest of bloggers and censorship of them. But that campaign fizzled when security agents pointed out that it was helping the democrats in their recruitment drive, while economists warned that attempts to neutralize the Internet would harm the economy at the very time it was experiencing mounting problems.

It was through the Internet, moreover, that thousands of Russians in the diaspora contributed to the growth of civil society back home. Here, again, popular pro-democratic uprisings in the Arab world came to mind. As one Russian analyst noted:

the participation of immigrants from Arab countries who were in Europe had an impact on the online agitation during the 'Arab Spring' and on the coverage of these events in the West. Immigrant bloggers created a sort of bridge that brought Western values and standards to their compatriots, who had no other opportunity to learn about democracy and human rights.[19]

Much the same thing was happening in Russia, and as the authorities lost their nerve, the dissidents became bolder and more relentless in demanding democratic reforms.

At the same time as the cosmopolitans ditched their Moscow-centric mindset, they discovered a large pool of talented and courageous leaders living outside the large cities who could articulate the dreams and grievances of their neighbors — if provided with the means to do so. This insight prompted the urban activists to collaborate with provincial leaders, and together they crafted alliances that the Kremlin could not ignore. Modest financial, legal, and organizational assistance enabled grassroots activists in the hinterland to construct community organizations that recruited people who previously had remained outside of politics. It was this specter that prompted Kremlin propagandists in 2012 to complain that Lithuania was providing venues for Western experts to train Russian agitators in the art of community organizing.

As was true of the Arab Spring, the young computer savvy generation and the growing legion of Russians in the diaspora introduced their elders to this new world of independent information. Of course, many of Russia's new rich vacationed in the West, had homes there, and favored American and European banks to protect their cash assets. They took comfort in the thought that should things get dicey for them at home, they could find refuge in London or Manhattan. If they chose exile, they would have to live in societies where the rule of law prevailed, but that was not a serious deterrent since many of them had learned how to use their wealth to protect their interests. They did so by buying the best legal talent in London or most politically wired public relations (PR) firms on K Street. American investigative reporters or enterprising analysts who uncovered malfeasance on the part of a Russian energy giant, for example, were silenced by a mere letter of warning from a powerful law firm in one of the Western capitals since they rarely had the financial heft to take on the oligarchs. Were Russia to become a truly pluralistic country, its new rich would have to take risks, but inaction would produce an even more uncertain future for them.

As more Kremlin insiders concluded their fate was tethered to the nation's best and brightest and disgruntled elements that were demanding change, Putin demonstrated his pragmatism and appointed Alexei Kudrin as Prime Minister. This surprised some Kremlin watchers since Kudrin openly denigrated some of Putin's most cherished policies. "I'm against the constant anti-Western rhetoric," he told a Spiegel interviewer, "even if it's only intended for domestic ears. It's detrimental to the modernization of our economy, and of course it doesn't help make Moscow a global financial center." And in spite of the crackdown, he observed that while there were no longer massive street demonstrations, "A new active civil society has developed."[20]

Henceforth, policies associated with economic and political revisionists were adopted: they included a stable ruble; checks on inflation; protecting property rights and contracts; fighting corruption; and reducing the country's defense budget. They also provided for free elections, the formation of opposition political parties, an independent media, effective anti-corruption measures and other major features prevalent in a law-based democratic polity. As these changes took place, domestic and foreign entrepreneurs began to invest in Russia while expanding existing joint ventures.

In sum, this pivot toward pluralism contributed to the appearance of a vibrant and expanding civil society, spearheaded by a pro-democracy movement that prompted even skeptics to conclude that Russia was on the road to pluralism. It did not appear overnight and encountered stiff crosswinds, but it took root over time because the Western path to development was the only one that provided change without bloodshed.

The International Prospect.

Several international developments helped reconfigure power relationships within Russia. In the aftermath of the USSR's demise, Putin had cited economic turmoil in the West to chastise rivals who championed American economic bromides. After all, the "bad years" of the 1990s were a product of Yeltsin's slavishly listening to American free market radicals that resulted in the 1998 crash. It, in turn, prompted a soft coup a year later when the Siloviki compelled Yeltsin to name Putin as his Prime Minister.

The George W. Bush administration demonstrated that American capitalism was corrupt and had fostered gross economic inequality and the worst international economic crisis since the Great Depression. It was responsible for a debt crisis that would plague the

American economy for a decade or more. Obama saw the economic challenge somewhat differently, but he, too, championed the free market and accommodated Wall Street before he turned to the ills of Main Street.

Europe's debt crisis, likewise, demonstrated the flaws of the EU and was responsible for unprecedented joblessness, declining public revenues, and plunging profits. Eventually economic stagnation would doom the "European project" and empower Euro-skeptics who demanded their nations break with the EU altogether. David Cameron, the United Kingdom's (UK) Prime Minister, was not the only European leader that harbored profound reservations about EU membership. At the same time, the new members from the East received a proportionately smaller share of development funds than the larger ones—so much for economic equality. Here again was further evidence that the Western model of development was outmoded and if Russia followed it, the outcome would be perilous.

Meanwhile, the world's most robust economy was thriving under the direction of men in Beijing that shared much in common with Putin regarding the "shortfalls" of Western-style democracy and capitalism. China enjoyed double-digit rates of growth for a quarter century, and its economy would soon be larger than its American counterpart. For many Russians who had reservations about liberal economic doctrine, the Chinese offered an alternative that many inside the Kremlin favored.

But as Russia encountered rough economic seas, a number of global developments occurred that challenged this condemnation of the West. For example, with a rebound in the American economy and expectations that by 2020 the United States would become energy independent, the campaign to denigrate the American modernization model lost credibility. Abundant energy in North America produced an upswing in manufacturing and a surge in other sectors resulting in dramatic job growth, escalating wages and plunging public debt. In spite of a protracted partisan dust-up over the debt crisis, investors worldwide once again saw the U.S. as a safe profit-making center.[21] Although the European recovery took longer, the creation of a true union with a strong central authority and associated economic institutions fostered a spike in economic activity throughout Europe. The process was painful, but the turnaround was predictable; after all, pundits proclaiming Europe's inevitable decline forgot that the EU was in competition with China and the United States for the title of "the world's largest economy." Under these circumstances, Russia's economic oligarchs and political leaders alike sought closer association with their European brethren.

This pivot was bolstered as the Chinese model lost its luster. The long-anticipated showdown between its energetic and expanding middle class and the communist Mandarins had commenced. Joined by a number of wealthy entrepreneurs and some revisionists in the Communist Party, they demanded a voice in political affairs that the leadership was not prepared to provide. To make matters worse, several hundred million displaced peasants who had entered the cities no longer were prepared to accept low wages and abysmal working conditions in silence. Numerous people had lost their jobs to low-wage workers elsewhere in Africa, Asia, and Central America, and their plight was another source of concern for the troubled communist leadership.

Ordinary citizens were especially outraged that the promises made by the new leaders in 2012 under the stewardship of Xi Jinping fell far short of their goals. In a growing number of instances, small entrepreneurs shuttered their enterprises and took to the streets to protest their corrupt leaders. Under these circumstances, violent protests became commonplace. They were given added weight by reports of desertions among the police and even in the People's Liberation Army (PLA). Foreign intelligence services indicated that the communist leadership ultimately had to give ground to demands among the middle class for real political influence, but many hardliners would not do so without a fight. In anticipation of that showdown, some analysts conjured up the prospects of mass revolt or a coup among the ruling elite.[22] These developments had a profound impact upon Russian fans of "the Chinese miracle." With growing unrest in China and the prospects of serious violent confrontation there, Russian hardliners lost a major rationale for their claim that the Western road to modernization was an economic dead end and a source of political instability.

Of course, globalization was the most consequential international development for Russia, but it was a two-edged sword. It had enhanced the life of the Power Vertical by producing a steady demand for energy exports, but it exposed the economy to disruptive international forces. With a dramatic uptick in alternative sources of gas and oil as exemplified by technological breakthroughs in North America, Russia faced stiff competition for its customers. This resulted in protracted economic difficulties that made it impossible for Moscow to intimidate its neighbors by playing the energy card. At the same time, without huge profit margins, the costs of corruption became even more difficult to ignore.

The democrats urged the Kremlin to take note. In the 21st century, no country could rely upon its own resources or policies to foster economic prosperity. Even the richest ones had to abide by the dictates of the marketplace and the rules of the international economic regimes that had emerged in the closing years of the 20th century. At the same time, there was reason for optimism; Russia possessed a vast storehouse of hydrocarbon wealth, arable land, clean water, and abundant minerals and timber. Its immense territory also served as an expanding crossroads of trade and transportation throughout Eurasia. What was missing was a modern polity that mobilized the masses behind a national campaign that enabled Russia to actualize its immense potential. In a word, a democratic, law-based polity would enhance the government's capacity to exploit all of these assets with the people's active support. Conversely, a march back toward autocracy was a dead end.

Here, then, was a road that promised prosperity and a foundation upon which a strong state rested. It would provide Russia with the opportunity to conduct its foreign relations from a position of strength, while at the same time exploit soft power as a useful diplomatic asset. Putin had been relentless in his campaign to enhance soft power, but he failed to realize that it and autocracy are mutually exclusive phenomenon. Clear-headed members of Russia's ruling elite realized that Moscow could not force its neighbors to surrender their sovereignty and suffer under Russian rule the way they did under the USSR. But Putin was right in that many of the countries identified with the Commonwealth of Independent States (CIS) remain attracted to the Russian language, Russian culture, and shared experiences that preceded the Soviet Empire. But he failed to acknowledge that Russia did not have to force itself upon its neighbors but rather let nature run its course, the same way that the Mexicans and Canadians came to grips with American power.[23]

On the other hand, a liberal Russia would have a significant and benign impact upon neighboring countries. In face of expanding Russian democracy, there would be a marked improvement in U.S.-Russian relations, making security cooperation on a range of matters plausible. For example, this could be an agreement covering the deployment of the American anti-missile system in Europe; curbing the proliferation of weapons of mass destruction (WMD); upgrading the New Start Treaty; resolving crises through the UN like those pertaining to Syria and Iran; stabilizing a post-U.S. 2014 Afghanistan; and moving toward Russia's membership in a new Euro-Atlantic security system.

Arguably this "best case" scenario does not represent the forecast of most Russian-watchers, but there is justification for it. A growing number of economic and political elites are now openly displaying reservations about the Power Vertical's capacity to survive. Similar conclusions prompted the Polish communists and later their Russian comrades to throw in the towel and not crush their opponents in a military Armageddon. The pivotal actors among the ruling class have not, as yet, made a decision about their next move. But as the younger generation gains access to economic and political centers of power, it is likely that a critical mass of the population will conclude that the status quo is unsustainable.

In spite of ominous trends, civil society is alive in Russia, and the cosmopolitans still feel comfortable attacking Putin and his colleagues. This is why Russia's democratic activists brush aside the present "dark days" and claim that real politics has taken root in their country and eventually those responsible for it will gain power as Russia retreats from autocracy. Many of Russia's most influential people, including some associated with the Power Vertical, are convinced that a more democratic political system will better enable Russia to actualize its huge economic potential. Should Russia move in this direction, the prospects for a rebalance in U.S.-Russian relations will improve dramatically, and that outcome will have a positive aspect upon an international system that faces multiple sources of instability and turbulence.

The Euro-Atlantic community can only help Russia achieve a democratic outcome on the margins, but it must find ways to work with the current leadership. The collapse of European communism was not a consequence of a hands-off policy but a by-product of internal forces and Western interaction with the communist Nomenklatura. Before Russia moves with purpose towards pluralism — and it will not happen overnight but step-by-step and will suffer some setbacks — it is likely to be preceded by a period of repression that exceeds the present status quo. This interregnum may be necessary since the coming of age of a new generation is one of the major preconditions for a pluralist Russia to take root. It is imperative then that the West maintain, nay dramatically increases, face-to-face interaction with ordinary Russians through cultural, educational and athletic events in addition to formal diplomatic and military-to-military channels.

STALIN LITE

The Domestic Aspect.

Putin was re-elected president in 2012 and the remaining Technocrats in the Kremlin were replaced by Siloviki hardliners. Russian-watchers claimed that henceforth, Putin would share power with them. They had endorsed his crackdown but claimed that he had not gone far enough in his war against "Russia's" enemies. As the economy faltered, they became even more critical of his stewardship and reasoned that he was incapable of effectively managing it. Claiming the country was facing a "national emergency," the new government adopted a system of rule that some observers labeled Stalin Lite—that is a quasi-police state.[24]

In truth, the major culprit was a steep free-fall in hydrocarbon revenues. Since they accounted for half of the state's income, the government was forced to slash salaries, pensions, and other public transfers. As an array of social service programs were cut, a rising tide of discontent erupted among a broad cross section of society. The rich and the privileged middle class—as was true in many Western countries—continued to enjoy security in face of growing economic inequality, occupied pockets of prosperity and enjoyed political clout that even the ruling elite could not ignore. But the rest of society saw a plunge in living standards. The most destitute were the 21st-century *Lumpernprolitariat*—victims of globalization and automation—who no longer possessed skills relevant to the modern world and could not survive on wages common in Africa, Asia, and parts of Latin America. Eventually, their anger spilled out into the streets in the form of strikes and violent actions that alarmed the Kremlin. In some instances, the police joined the protestors in demanding higher wages and better benefits of their own.

As the defense budget suffered considerable hits, the Kremlin was alarmed by protests from the armed forces and civilian members of the military-industrial complex. Under these circumstances, many Siloviki concluded that Putin had lost his grip and something dramatic had to be done to stabilize the situation. In what some observers depicted as a return to a "command economy," the government tightened control of business, financial, and commercial practices. The priority was no longer growth or vain attempts at economic diversification but stability and control. Foreign critics said by returning to a police state, the Siloviki were living in a fantasy world as these odious measures would only make things worse.

Meanwhile, on the political front, liberals, some leftists, and anti-Kremlin nationalists were being arrested and imprisoned in expanding numbers, while others who had not reached an accommodation with the Kremlin chose exile or refuge in silence. Some observers predicted that repression would backfire; the people were no longer afraid and would respond in massive protests. The authorities responsible for this new more odious crackdown were simply out of touch with the mood of the country. Kremlin officials responded that it was the Western-oriented democrats who lived in a bubble of their own. They had been so seduced by pronouncements on the part of the Western media — "Putin's days are numbered" and "the people are no longer afraid" — that they ignored recent historical lessons to the contrary. Repression works! Recall in effect Stalin's remark: "[E]liminate the agitator, and the problem goes away." Conversely, it was the failure of the hardliners in the Communist Party of the Soviet Union (CPSU) to destroy Perestroika in its crib that set in motion a stream of events that culminated in the Soviet Empire's implosion. The Siloviki in the 21st century would not make the same mistake.

Perhaps Putin's days were numbered but not those of his compatriots who were quarterbacking the crackdown. Furthermore, the malcontents that brazenly took to the streets earlier now were cowed into silence. Like their parents and grandparents, they were duly afraid of the mailed fist. The problem had been that Putin had been too timid in deploying it, but those now in charge would not make the same mistake. Long anticipated pesky opponents like Navalny and Udalstov were put in jail on trumped-up criminal charges. They were joined by hundreds of other leading opposition figures, and courageous journalists were being killed in a new round of assassinations that presumably were being conducted by members of organized crime or government agents—frequently, it was impossible to differentiate between the two. Most ordinary folk in Russia accepted these measures without comment.

Ethnic Russians in particular did so because they feared the violence that had reached new levels of mayhem in the North Caucasus would spread into Russia proper. In the aftermath of Assad's fall in Syria, Russian security officials discovered that many citizens from the North Caucasus that had fought in Syria now were helping indigenous jihadists create a Caucasus Caliphate, and they were being joined by foreign terrorists as well. When the newly emboldened Kremlin rulers embarked upon a campaign to crush the insurgencies in the North Caucasus, they were applauded by most ethnic Russians.

More and more insurgents had embraced the Green of Islam. As was the case of earlier military operations, this one resulted in wholesale human rights violations and heavy civilian casualties. In justification, the authorities reminded the public that in addition to the violence that these terrorist conducted in their own region, they were responsible for bombing trains and buildings in Russia proper — including Moscow and St. Petersburg.

Earlier, Putin had responded to this unrest by adopting a modest form of nation building — but the funds earmarked for that endeavor in Chechnya, Dagestan, Ingushetia, and other entities in the region did not help the people who needed assistance. As Navalny had claimed, much of the money was stolen by local mobsters and their Russian confederates.

The violent upheaval in southern Russia, however, gave rise to a new development: the creation of Slavic-nationalist "fighting groups." The expanding Islamic jihad facilitated the resurrection of Cossacks in areas near the Volga and other places where Russians and Muslims lived in close proximity to one another. But now paramilitary organizations, with help from local police and military units, were flourishing and uniting around an anti-Islamic agenda. Intercommunal enmity had been fed by the Kremlin's campaign to fold ethnic political entities into larger ones to minimize the influence of non-Russian groups. But it backfired and gave ethnic separatists ammunition to take on Russian chauvinism. Along a parallel path, the Kremlin bankrolled indigenous leaders — most notably the Chechen Ramzan Kadyrov — to enlist their support in the struggle against the jihadists. They did so with relentless brutality and in fact served as a recruiting tool for the jihadists and other insurgents operating in minority communities in many parts of Russia.

This scenario had its origins in the split that first attracted international attention in the fall of 2011 when Putin took back the presidency and left Medvedev twisting in the wind. A year later, after the younger man was pilloried in anonymous videos—among other things for supporting the UN resolution that condoned the Libyan bombing campaign conducted by NATO—pundits reported the end of the "tandem." Kremlin insiders claimed Putin was convinced that Medvedev had betrayed him by collaborating with the very Technocrats and middle class liberals that were subverting the Power Vertical.[25]

At the same time, Putin claimed the Technocrats were collaborating with foreign (read American) agents who were seeking to subvert Russia. This was an attempt to reclaim the support of those provincials that had expressed doubt about Putin's capacity to rule in their behalf. His penchant for scapegoating was not new; he did the same thing after the Beslan School massacre in North Ossetia when he linked the Chechen insurgents—responsible for the outrage—to unnamed foreign enemies. They were not only bent on undermining Putin but destroying "Russia itself."[26]

Here, then, was an attempt on Putin's part to purge from his team anyone who did not demonstrate unqualified loyalty to him, while at the same time striving to regain the trust of those ordinary folk that remained tethered to Soviet-style enterprises or who lived by sufferance of State entitlements. He hoped to achieve this two-part objective by creating a new popular front movement that replaced what remained of the Power Vertical with a new regime that enhanced his capacity to rule. Toward this end, he promoted an ultra-nationalist Slavic narrative that celebrated Russia's magnificent past exploits. The campaign began on December 12, 2012, when he delivered a state of the nation address at the resplendent St. George Hall in the Grand Kremlin Palace. "Putin barely mentioned the outside world," but said that Russians needed "to turn inward" and:

> look to patriotism, not Westernism; to solidarity, not individualism; to spirituality, not consumerism and moral decay. He touted Russia's historic roots and traditional values as the basis for its future trajectory.[27]

Democracy was the only political choice for Russia, but it rested on "the power of the Russian people with their own traditions of self-rule and not the fulfillment of standards imposed on us from the outside."[28] To protect his political flank, he was banking on deeply rooted cultural values, historical experiences, and religious impulses associated with Slavic ultra-nationalism, the Orthodox Church, and centuries of imperial rule that elevated all ethnic Russians. He reasoned the Russian people would embrace the existential imperatives of community, not the abstractions of reason that enthralled the urban liberals. Earlier, Putin neither encouraged the nationalists nor vilified the country's large Muslim population, but in one of his first public events at the Presidential Palace in 2012, he appeared in a photo-op with a Russian heavy metal motorcycle gang that celebrated the Russian Orthodox faith. In their lyrics, they attacked Muslims in the most brutal terms imaginable.[29] Moreover, while the Moscow intelligentsia excoriated him for endorsing the Pussy Riot rock group's 2-year jail sentence, polls indicated that most Russians favored it. From the perspective of the ultra-nationalists with whom the Siloviki had found common cause, the only problem was that Putin did not go far enough in "putting the minorities in their place."

But they also cited Putin's temerity in not crushing the Russian regional elites that had established virtual independent fiefdoms from Vladivostok in the Far East to Kaliningrad in the Far West. In Siberia, political leaders in conjunction with local business interests were snubbing federal authorities, and some members of the regional police and military units were actively collaborating with them. Simultaneously, Omon-type units were being deployed in border regions where the population was vulnerable to foreign influences. In this connection, Kaliningrad, the Western most oblast that is surrounded by Lithuania and Poland, was considered by security operatives uniquely sensitive to "outside provocation."[30]

Finally, the government turned to the cosmopolitans and their most powerful weapon, the Internet. In conjunction with "smart phones," it was an unrivalled recruiting tool that enabled them to disseminate their "subversive" pro-Western narrative throughout Russia. As a consequence, a nationwide campaign to "purge" the Internet was undertaken: it involved censorship, the closing of portals, and the arrest of bloggers. The number accused of political crimes tripled from 2011 to 2012. The campaign silenced many of them, while others fled the country or disconnected their computers.[31] The newest campaign would take even more draconian measures to emasculate the Internet and associated technology such as "smart phones."

Even so, tens of thousands of Russians that lived in the diaspora — in tech savvy localities like Silicon Valley, California, and Fairfax, Virginia, as well as throughout Europe — conducted a "truth telling" campaign to counteract the Kremlin's disinformation blitz. Their ability to communicate in Russian was of special concern to the Siloviki because most ordinary folk in Russia were not fluent in English. It was with similar concerns in mind that the authorities turned toward foreign affairs with even greater zeal than did Putin. It was a blogger in Spain — Dr. Z — who revealed that Vladimir Pekhtin, a Duma representative, had property in Miami, Florida, that eventually led to his ouster from that body.[32] In turn, his fate gave impetus to Putin's decision to order government officials to return all of their foreign assets to Russia. In doing so, Putin could anticipate alienating many of the same people who had been his most steadfast supporters.

The International Prospect.

Under these circumstances, prospects for a re-balance in U.S.-Russia relations were hobbled. While realists urged President Obama to cooperate with Russia on matters of mutual concern — fighting terrorism, curbing the proliferation of WMD, etc. — anti-Russian sentiment soared among members of Congress and human rights activists. White House political advisers and policymakers were at odds over this matter, since the former argued that the domestic political costs of any effort to cooperate with Moscow exceeded the anticipated international benefits.

What had been called a "crackdown on steroids" produced much the same reaction in European capitals. Berlin and Moscow had enjoyed a "special relationship" for years so that members of Germany's Social Democratic Party and Christian Democratic Party alike had kept silent in face of the most odious behavior emanating from Russia. This largely reflected the power of the German business community that relied upon Russia for energy and in return saw it as a customer hungry for German products. But ever since Chancellor Angela Merkel scolded Putin for his human rights violations in late-2012, the relationship cooled considerably. The rest of Europe pretty much reacted the same way to developments in Russia. As the Europeans depended less upon Russia's energy, animosity toward the Kremlin prompted some seasoned observers to proclaim a new cold war was in the works.[33]

Moscow's aggressive behavior toward the countries occupying the former Soviet space was another source of concern in the West. Efforts to reintegrate — or what former Secretary Clinton called "re-Sovietize" — Belarus and Ukraine were dramatically accelerated by Moscow. Minsk and Kiev, wracked by economic problems and political turmoil, could not refuse Russian orders to snub the West. They needed the Russians more than the other way around, and here was evidence of the Putin Doctrine at work. In addition to maintaining its superpower nuclear status, Russia sought "regional hegemony" that involved "political, economic, military, and cultural reintegration of the former Soviet bloc." An important element here was the campaign to enforce "Finlandization" upon the countries formerly tied to the USSR.[34] They could conduct their domestic affairs any way they wished, but their foreign relations had to conform to the dictates of the Russian foreign ministry.

Russian-Georgian relations took a turn for the worse, and some observers talked openly about a replay of the Five-Day War. Russian officials claimed that Georgians once closely aligned with Saakashvili were now actively supporting jihadists in Russia. His replacement, Bidzina Ivanishvili, tried to placate the Russians, but his courting NATO membership was cited by officials in Moscow as evidence of his "double-dealing."

Even though Ukrainian government favored close relations with Moscow and its leadership and people alike rejected NATO membership, the Kremlin was not happy about Kiev's bid for EU membership. As a consequence of the Siloviki victory, the Kremlin demanded Kiev not deviate from the policies that were favored in Moscow.

Officials in Baku likewise claimed that Russian provocateurs were encouraging the Armenians in Nagorno-Karabakh to provoke new violent confrontations with the pro-American Azeri government. Since Russia supported the Armenians and Turkey supported the Azeris, this frozen conflict threatened to do serious harm to relations between Moscow and Istanbul. At the same time, there were many influential voices in Moscow that saw closer relations with Tehran as a counterpoint to the American-Turkish campaign to compromise Russia's interests in its "own back yard."

Imperialistic utterances from Moscow prompted expressions of alarm throughout the "near abroad." Kremlin security agents became bolder in fomenting political discord in all of them, while Moscow exploited its economic assets to subvert members of the local business community and media.[35] After all, the Siloviki claimed the Lithuanians were conducting workshops to help provocateurs undermine Russia's government. Along with Poland, it was a base for Belorussians who were plotting regime change in their old homeland. In response, Lithuanian authorities lobbied Brussels and Washington to reaffirm NATO's Article Five obligations and bolster defenses throughout Eastern Europe.

In this frigid environment, the perceived linkage between Russia's internal problems and the U.S. campaign to promote regime change encouraged the Kremlin to obstruct American foreign policy priorities — like those favoring radical change in the Greater Middle East. Therefore Moscow demonstrated special sensitivity when the Americans sought international justification to intimidate the Mullahs in Tehran. The military cited America's "aggressive and subversive" foreign initiatives to justify a dramatic hike in defense spending. Their civilian masters needed no encouragement when the campaign to sustain Russia's nuclear strike force was mentioned. Money was tight, but Russia's very survival depended upon its nuclear deterrent. Likewise, it was unconscionable to deny funding for general purpose forces. The army, air, and naval arms all had to be upgraded to the point where foreign enemies could not assume a military strike against Russia would go unpunished.

Thinking along these lines was an asset to those hawks in the Kremlin who looked upon heavy defense spending as an economic force multiplier. In a word, the road to a growing diversified economy. Of course, this bogus notion was popular among the Soviet Nomenklatura, and the technocrats warned that it would do grave harm to Russia's economy in the 21st century the same way it did to the Soviet economy in the 20th century. Earlier, Putin had been warned that his rearmament drive that amounted to "$700 billion over a decade without first developing a security and defense strategy that" was "aligned with 21st-century realities" was a major blunder.[36] At the same time, the army's drive for heavy defense spending rested on the principle of deterrence, not domination. In event of another Georgian war, the West — including the

Americans — would have to think twice about providing reckless provocateurs like Saakashvili with weapons. Russia did not welcome a military confrontation with NATO, but it wanted to make any aggressor pay a price so heavy that it would avoid a confrontation with Russian forces in the first place — not to defeat them in a conventional war.

Of course, intemperate accusations from Russian officials prompted expressions of outrage in Washington and gave rise to demands in Congress for the United States to re-deploy U.S. air, ground, and naval units in Eastern Europe. Many in the American media and think tanks openly proclaimed the onset of a "new cold war." Whatever measures the White House took, any hope of cooperating with Russia on security matters were dashed. EU officials and their counterparts in Europe's major capitals likewise expressed alarm about Russia's quick-march back toward Stalinist-like policies.

The crackdown and scapegoating, however, only contributed to Russia's dysfunctional image, resulting in a massive pullback in capital on the part of both domestic and international investors. Predictably, this reaction plunged the economy into a deeper morass. To compensate, revenues originally earmarked for social welfare programs were redirected toward a burgeoning defense budget.

As fears about a serious insurgency soared, the Kremlin leadership became even more sensitive to "efforts on the part of foreign enemies" to exploit the situation. Officials in various government think-tanks produced papers providing "evidence" that U.S. "black services" were supporting the jihadists just as they did in subverting Assad in Syria and Mubarak in Egypt. Under these circumstances, it was ludicrous to prattle about a rebalance of U.S.-Russian relations.

Nonetheless, the overlords in the Kremlin were acute enough to realize that the correlation of forces favored the West and not the hobbled resurrected Russian state in any military showdown. Tough rhetoric aside, they neither had the means nor the will to act upon their threats to engage their neighbors in violent confrontations. That said, many analysts feared that the hawks in Moscow might mistakenly believe that they knew where the red lines were—lines that they would never cross lest they provoke a violent clash with their neighbors and their Western protectors.

There was also a contentious debate raging in Russia's defense establishment about joining the PLA in a truly effective security relationship. Some argued against this option since it would mean Russia would serve as the junior partner. But others noted that Russia's nuclear strike force would make it at the very least an equal partner in the enterprise. This was especially the case when the generals in the PLA considered that serious discussions were taking place in defense circles in Seoul, South Korea, and Tokyo, Japan, about South Korea and Japan building their own nuclear arsenals since they could no longer depend upon the American deterrent. With Russia's nuclear arsenal as a force multiplier, the PLA would have a formidable counterweight in Beijing's protracted competition with the Americans.

Whatever the prospects for a Chinese-Russian security arrangement, proponents of a re-balance in relations with Russia had to answer a compelling question: How could any American administration find avenues of security cooperation with Moscow in this toxic environment?

RUSSIA IN CHAOS: THE WORST CASE SCENARIO

The Domestic Prospect.

Kremlin-watchers agree that the days of the Power Vertical and Putin's rule are numbered, and Russian society is about to face significant internal political disruptions.[37] The people running things in Russia, however, appear to be ill-prepared to deal with them. Likewise, the last time Russia faced a "formidable challenge to its great power ambitions" was about 3 centuries ago. In the end, Russia survived this "time of troubles" and actually expanded its empire. But this time, Russian-watchers predict the Kremlin leadership will prove incapable of imposing its will upon Russia's foreign rivals and, worse yet, may face a new internal crisis that results in a fate similar to that of the USSR.

In the aftermath of the Soviet Union's breakup, many leaders, Putin among them, feared Russia might go the way of Yugoslavia and fragment into a number of parts. But today, few foreign analysts believe Russia will break apart or experience widespread violence bordering on civil war. Many deem talk of this nature as simply foolhardy. Leonid Radzikhovsky is one of them; he dismisses predictions of Russia's disintegration implausible since most of its residents are ethnic Russians who represent about 70 percent of the population, and they recoil at the idea that Russia will be the subject of Balkanization à la Yugoslavia. Most minority ethnic groups or political enterprises like Tatarstan cannot function as viable economic and political entities without Russian help. Those that reside on borders with foreign countries such as China cannot rely upon Beijing's help in breaking free of Russian rule. On the contrary, like their rival in Washington, the leadership in Beijing has little stomach for Russia's fragmentation. It would have exceedingly ominous consequence for the United States and China alike as the shock waves it promulgated would destabilize a world already in a state of disorder and existential peril. Also, any attempt to openly encourage Russians to turn against their own leaders would be foolhardy, given Russia's massive WMD arsenal.[38]

American analysts who deem serious internal strife and political chaos in Russia implausible, however, must consider all possible outcomes, especially those that have the potential of profoundly changing the international security picture. Currently, analysts worry about jihadists securing WMD in Syria and Pakistan that could be used against neighboring countries or even the United States. But neither possesses the vast arsenal of biological weapons, chemical agents, and nuclear weapons, along with sophisticated delivery systems, that Russia does. Fears about Russia cascading into chaos then justify serious study, even if most analysts believe it implausible. Recall how few members of the American security community believed an attack akin to September 11, 2001 (9/11) was plausible? Also remember that the vast majority of American security analysts failed to anticipate the breakup of the Soviet Empire.

Soon after Gorbachev became General Secretary of the CPSU in 1985, national security experts in Washington rallied around four perspectives:

1. *The Soviet Leviathan.* With the publication of George F. Kennan's historic *Sources of Soviet Conduct* in 1947, the major concern of U.S. strategists rested on the fear that the Warsaw Pact would overrun the

NATO defenders—even if they did not resort to tactical nuclear weapons as was their intention. Subsequently, realists argued that what happened within the USSR was of little consequence, what mattered most was its capacity to project its power internationally. Moreover, even conceding it confronted serious economic, ethnic, and political problems, the notion that the Soviet Empire would be brought down as a result of "internal contradictions" was unthinkable. The analysts who eventually became known as the neo-conservatives, and deemed Richard Nixon's policy of détente disastrous, were of the same opinion. The Kremlin overlords enjoyed a monopoly of power—the Red Army, KGB, and militia—so they would have little difficulty crushing the dissidents.

In failing to anticipate the Soviet Union's collapse, both camps committed a monumental intellectual error. They were not alone; prominent American statesmen like Henry Kissinger deemed the USSR's disintegration a fantasy and only a minority of his colleagues—most notably Zbigniew Brzezinski—believed otherwise. Jimmy Carter's former national security chief was among the minority that correctly predicted that the "nationalities question" was the USSR's Achilles heel. Gorbachev forgot that and lost an empire.[39]

2. *Hardliners Would Replace Gorbachev*. By 1991, as Perestroika exacerbated the very problems it was designed to resolve, the George H. W. Bush administration feared Gorbachev would be replaced by hardliners who favored a reaffirmation of Stalinist policies and not liberal reforms. In an attempt to save Gorbachev—and, in effect, the Soviet Empire—President George H. W. Bush flew to Kiev where he pleaded with the

Ukrainians not to leave "Gorbie" in a lurch and join a new truncated union that was under discussion. This desertion of what Ronald Reagan had championed under the rubric "rollback" prompted William Safire of *The New York Times* to characterize Bush's words as the "Chicken-Kiev" speech.[40] Bush was credited for not humiliating Gorbachev's successors but had he anticipated the USSR's collapse, perhaps Washington would have been better prepared to deal with the aftermath of this staggering historical event—specifically, taking steps to eventually integrate Russia into a post-Cold War European security system.

3. *An Impotent Russia Tethered To The West.* A more benign view of post-Soviet Russia prevailed in Washington after the collapse of Soviet imperialism in Eastern Europe, the free-fall in the Red Army's capabilities, the subsequent dramatic decline in population and territory and profound economic difficulties that culminated in the 1998 crash.[41] In a word, Russia was no longer an existential threat even though it possessed a massive nuclear arsenal. Programs like the Nunn-Lugar initiative helped ameliorate the misuse of the Soviet nuclear arsenal and, more recently, so did the New Start Treaty. Furthermore, Russia's leaders were preoccupied with the daunting task of rebuilding a country riven by a host of serious internal challenges.

After cooperating with Russia in some areas, the George H. Bush administration alarmed the Kremlin by scrapping the ABM Treaty—and, following Bill Clinton's example, expanded NATO eastward; subsequently, relations between both countries cooled. In 2009, Obama forged a reset in relations that resulted in the New Start Treaty and expansion of the Northern Distribution Network that was vital to the American military campaign in Afghanistan, but by 2012, the reset was deemed moribund. Indeed, a year earlier, Russia was only mentioned briefly in the Joint Chiefs National Military Strategy document.

> We seek to co-operate with Russia on counter-terrorism, counter-proliferation, space, and ballistic missile defense, and welcome it playing a more active role in preserving security and stability in Asia.[42]

Russian commentators complained that Russia was mentioned as a sub-text to the principle American preoccupation — Asia.

During his first term as president and in spite of his tough rhetoric, Putin believed Russia's fate rested upon a harmonious relationship with the Americans. By 2007, Putin changed his tune when he proclaimed at Munich that the "unipolar moment" — i.e., when the Americans dictated to the world — was over. Henceforth, Russia had to be treated like an equal, not a supplicant, but he reasoned the prospects for fruitful cooperation were slim, so he passed the Western portfolio over to his young sidekick, Medvedev. In focusing on Putin's remarks, however, many observers overlook two pertinent observations: first, in that same address, Putin indicated that he wanted to work with Bush in stemming the proliferation of nuclear weapons; and second, in Russia's 2012 foreign policy concept a working relationship with the West is acknowledged as a priority.[43]

4. *The Breakup of the Soviet Empire and Armageddon.* In 1993, as the last Russian trucks rumbled through the streets of old town Vilnius, Lithuania, one displayed a sign with four ominous words: "WE WILL

BE BACK!" This prospect was not ignored by Lithuania's leaders who feared that in the near future a return of Russian tanks was a real prospect. Many of their neighbors harbored the same nightmare, but some observers deemed this scenario less likely than a more existential threat. Russia would implode much as the Soviet Empire did, only this time with violent outbreaks throughout the country, and the subsequent turbulence would spread to the Baltic democracies since many revanchists in Moscow claimed all three were part of Russia's patrimony.

This fourth perspective represented a minority view and did not receive the attention that it deserved. Yet there were a number of reasons why Russia could follow the Soviet example:

- The daunting challenge of succession was unresolved;
- The centrifugal forces of ethnic separatism was a real prospect as the insurgencies in the North Caucasus flourished and the Muslims that represented almost 20 percent of the population became disgruntled with Russian rule;
- The military was demoralized and in disarray as enlisted men and many officers and their families lived in squalor;
- The criminal organizations that thrived under the USSR now openly operated in collusion with the Siloviki and the oligarchs; and,
- The vast majority of ordinary people were as powerless as they were during Soviet rule.

And, of course, the man who was president, Boris Yeltsin, was an aging drunk with chronic heart disease who was incapable of managing the economy. Under these circumstances, there was a real prospect that Russia would implode, and it almost did on several occasions.

In October 1993, after President Yeltsin disbanded the Parliament, Vice-President Alexander Rutskoi led the fight against this "abuse of power." He had the support of communists and nationalists, but the Army surrounded the White House with tanks and fired upon the rebels, forcing them to surrender. The tank commanders decided to do so after several days of hesitation and only after Yeltsin mobilized the citizens of Moscow in opposing Rutskoi and his supporters. Given the president's grassroots support, any units that were prepared to side with the Vice-President ran the risk of a violent outbreak that could consume the entire country. According to official reports, 146 people were killed and 1,000 wounded during the conflict. But the bloodletting could have been far worse and the outcome truly disastrous.

Later, Yeltsin's selection of the Siloviki's favorite for Prime Minister — Vladimir Putin — was a result of a silent coup. Had Yeltsin refused to bend to pressure from the military and security services, no one knows what the outcome would have been but something akin to a military putsch could not be discounted.

Fast forward to the present and as a consequence of events and policies that were highlighted in the Stalin Lite scenario, Russia lapses into chaos. The major catalyst is an economic downturn as hydrocarbon rents nosedive and other sectors of the economy stagnate while domestic and foreign investors flee the country. Henceforth, the Kremlin cannot provide workers "living wages," while those in the old Soviet-style industries face the blight of unemployment. The plight of pensioners, and those individuals who rely upon government entitlements, result in unprecedented economic hardship and spawn massive protests among the provincials.

The picture becomes even darker when the Kremlin is informed that the "demographic time bomb" that demographers earlier had speculated about had become a reality. Russian women were having babies in ever smaller numbers, while the working-age population was shrinking. The estimate that Russia would lose 26 million productive citizens by 2050 appeared to be on target.

Meanwhile, the flow of funds to the military and security services had become problematic, and orders for new weapons and equipment were cancelled. As the supply of 18-year-old recruits slumped, it became ever more difficult to recruit capable soldiers. Under these circumstances, some members of the officer corps seek salvation in alliances with economic warlords, criminal gangs, and ultra-nationalist organizations that have mushroomed in the face of economic hardship, social upheaval, and a dysfunctional political system.

At the same time, the Kremlin leadership is incapable of dealing with events since the clans are at war with one another, and at times the conflict has resulted in violent clashes between them. Without Putin, the oligarchs and other powerful players in Russian society no longer have a referee to establish and enforce rules that rationalize business deals—with the predictable outcome being chaos. Moreover, the perpetual struggle between the elites in the center and those in the provinces has taken on a new intensity as regional business and political leaders in the hinterland now operate like independent entities. The flow of commodities and resources from the provinces no longer can be taken for granted by the overlords in

Moscow. It was with this fear in mind that in 2004 Putin adopted policies that denied local constituents the opportunity to choose their governors.

To make matters worse, there is an uptick in the quantity and quality of armed insurgencies being waged within Russia. They are not only limited to the North Caucasus where religious fanaticism has replaced nationalistic impulses as the motivating force for violence. Armed groups that appear in minority communities have facilitated the formation of Cossack fighting units and like-minded ultra-Slavic nationalist entities that are supported by nervous members of the Kremlin elite.

As these developments unfold, the White House national security team calls a special session after receiving the following terse message from the American Ambassador in Moscow: "The ruling elite are badly divided. Expect Armageddon!" In return, he receives the following response from the White House: "Who is in charge?" and "Are the WMD safe?"

One observation that has a bearing on both questions is that while the people in charge under Stalin Lite embarked upon aggressive rhetoric and at times took measures that made their neighbors nervous, they judiciously honored Red Lines. They were not foolish enough to engage in confrontations that would lead to a military showdown with NATO.

But the motley collection of warlords, ethnic insurgent leaders, mafia crime bosses, and those heading regional fiefdoms often ignored Red Lines or proved incapable of controlling their fractious followers. Even more alarming, since the military's command structure collapsed, American intelligence doubted the authorities could deny insurgents access to the vast inventory of nuclear weapons, tactical as well as strategic ones—along with delivery systems—not to mention the lethal arsenal of biological agents and chemical weapons that Russia possesses. Even if the WMD were safe, the availability of a vast storehouse of conventional arms would provide undisciplined armed factions with the firepower to wage civil war.

The International Prospect.

The Eurasian Economic Union's disintegration was a cruel blow for the Kremlin. It was designed to snatch Armenia, Azerbaijan, Belarus, Georgia, and Ukraine from the clutches of the EU's Eastern Partnership program by offering alternative trade and commercial opportunities that Brussels dangled before them. Putin first embarked upon the venture with his sights set on Belarus and Kazakhstan since both depended upon Russia's energy and pipelines and sought access to a market of 143 million people. But not far into his term, Putin used his formidable economic clout to force Ukraine and Moldova into the Union. It provided the Kremlin with a geo-political architecture consistent with Russia's campaign to project its power throughout most of the former Soviet space—priority number one of the 2012 foreign policy concept.

According to American analysts, a week after Putin proclaimed that he would run for the presidency in 2012, he:

> . . . announced his desire for Russia to again lead a multinational bloc of tightly bound, former Soviet Republics. But major obstacles stand in the way of Putin's project, and the prospects of a new Eurasian Union emerging any time soon in the former Soviet space are small.[44]

Given mounting economic problems within all of the member states and pandemic corruption, lawlessness and Russia's contempt for the junior partners, the Union unraveled. It represented a major economic setback for the Siloviki and their business associates and precipitated a bitter and at times violent struggle to secure control of a shrinking pie. It also undermined the Kremlin's campaign to thrust Russia before the world again as a major international force.

In the Ukraine, a country the size of France with a population of 46 million, the leadership was divided, and turbulence originating in Russia ignited a violent confrontation between its warring factions. At the same time, there were clashes between well-armed ethnic Russians and Ukrainian nationalists in many places, and in the Crimea what remained of the Tatar population attacked Russian naval units. At the same time, criminal clans representing disparate ethnic communities were involved in violent confrontations that fed the flames of discord throughout the country.

In the case of Belarus, Alexander Lukashenka resorted to even more violent means to crush democratic activists and to intimidate ordinary citizens. In contrast to the past, this campaign of brutal suppression prompted a backlash, and the violence threatened to spill over into Lithuania and Poland.

In Russia's Far East, foreign revanchists were encouraging Russian and minority elites to break with Moscow and enjoy de facto, if not de jure, independence. In short, predictions that Russia would someday lose control of territory "East of the Urals" were no longer delusional.

A Russia on the verge of collapse prompted some in Beijing to consider how China might exploit its neighbor's time of troubles. Some intelligence analysts in the West concluded that, while China coveted this prized territory, the PLA was not unmindful of Yeltsin's remark that, while Russia's "nuclear-tipped rockets were rusty, they worked." While the Russians were preoccupied with their own internal problems, the Chinese set their sights on Central Asia where they helped puppets of Beijing crush their political opponents. That was no easy task since jihadists in all five countries, encouraged by Russia's preoccupation with its own internal challenges, were conducting insurgencies with the expectation of victory and the creation of a single Central Asian Caliphate.

To complicate the security picture, sectarian violence erupted in many cities which attracted non-Russian migrants from many parts of the former Soviet Union. In Moscow, ethnic Russians clashed with Muslim migrants from the Caucasus and Central Asia. Consequently, jihadist leaders concluded that the time was ripe to create an Islamist Caliphate within Russia's borders; that is, one that far exceeded in ambition like-minded efforts that already operated there.

In addition to providing arms, ammunition, and money to indigenous jihadists, fighters from throughout the Greater Middle East were now infiltrating into Russia in significant numbers. At the same time, they were responsible for a frenzy of bombings and assassinations in major Russian cities and destroyed vital economic targets like pipelines, pumping stations, rail tracks, and power networks.

The Russian military—whose ranks were filled with disgruntled enlisted and officer personnel—were incapable of stabilizing the situation. They lacked sufficient communications equipment, vehicles, appropriate aircraft, and weapon systems to suppress the insurgents. In a growing number of instances, the insurgents employed tactics that bled American forces in Iraq and Afghanistan and, when necessary, found safe havens in neighboring Islamic countries. It was obvious that they hoped to provoke violent confrontations between Russian and Western units in areas of the former Soviet space just as their compatriots had successfully done in setting off Sunnis and Shiites in the Greater Middle East.

In conclusion, a Russia stricken by the collapse of central authority, resulting in de facto, if not de jure, fragmentation of the regime along with other dislocations may constitute the least plausible scenario but should it materialize, the consequences for the international order will be monumental. Stricken by a power vacuum, something approaching anarchism cannot be discounted along with the proliferation of ethnic, religious, regional, and economic fiefdoms that replace centralized authority in Russia. The new lines of authority, then, are horizontal, not vertical. This is one of the major features of the turmoil that has appeared throughout the greater Middle East, and much the same thing could happen in Russia. For this reason alone, U.S. planners must pay serious attention to it. Since this scenario is deemed unthinkable, a number of controversial questions regarding Russian relations have not been part of public discourse, but they deserve our attention:

- Were this scenario to materialize, how would the United States and its NATO allies respond to this colossal event? In considering intervention, we might consider the mistakes that we made in the Greater Middle East: namely, the jihadist threat was only a part of a far larger historical development—a civil war within Islam that could only be resolved by the 1.3 billion members of the Islamic Umma, not by outsiders. The lesson: let the Russians resolve their own crises.[45]

- Arguably, the most compelling rational for intervention is prompted by the question:
- Could the United States stand by and allow jihadist fanatics, irrational ultra-nationalists, and undisciplined nonstate actors secure control of Russia's massive nuclear arsenal and associated chemical and biological weapons—not to mention its vast arsenal of conventional weapons?
- How would the West respond to requests from Russian authorities that they required outside help to prevent their WMD from falling into the "wrong hands?" Would it choose sides in the hope of producing an outcome favorable to the victory of pluralist interests or would it—fearing a disastrous entanglement—remain as an interested but hesitant bystander?
- How would the United States respond to intrusions on the part of foreign agents or countries seeking to seize control of Russia's WMD or parts of its territory? Would it respond unilaterally or through NATO or the UN? Is it plausible to include China in such an enterprise and if not, what role might Beijing play in this unthinkable event?

CONCLUSIONS AND RECOMMENDATIONS

The Final Word on Putin and the Power Vertical.

Some analysts would argue that Russia has left behind the Status Quo scenario, and that Putin's crackdown justifies the claim that the Stalin Lite alternative better represents conditions in Russia today. The evidence is mounting that there are bad days ahead for Russia's one-legged economy as profits for gas and oil along with commodity prices are problematic. Without a steady supply of revenues, Putin can neither meet the promises he has made to workers and pensioners nor to members of the military industrial complex. Efforts to diversify the economy have produced limited results, and Putin has no plans in place to address the myriad roadblocks to a law-based free market economy. Prospects for economic growth will slip even further as both domestic and foreign investors, hounded by corruption and lawlessness, withdraw money from Russia.

Putin is attempting to reconfigure his political base by turning to the church, Slavic nationalism, and a celebration of Mother Russia, but most analysts believe that ultimately he will fail to stabilize a society in turmoil. He may adopt even harsher repressive measures to silence the democrats, purge his inner circle, and craft a new political order. But as the Siloviki and clans lose confidence in him, he will be neutralized or removed from power.

That said, Putin's demise may be years in the future. While the Power Vertical can survive without him, the Siloviki surge further toward the autocratic right, banking the regime's survival upon Russian nationalism, the church, and a successful campaign to portray the cosmopolitans as agents of the United States and carriers of alien values. A climate of fear among them, and pervasive apathy among the provincials, will allow the hardliners to survive for some time.

Russian-watchers mention a number of people who are likely successors of Putin: Deputy Prime Minister Dmitry Rogozin; Sergei Ivanov, the Kremlin Chief of Staff; Sergey Shoigu, the Defense Minister; and Igor Sechin, the head of Rosneft. It is noteworthy that Sechin has been called the "second most powerful man in Russia." He has worked closely with his "boss" ever since the St. Petersburg days and now is the chief executive officer for the oil giant, Rosneft. After Khorokovsky was sent to prison, Yukos was folded into Rosneft and as a consequence of buying out British Petroleum's oil investments, the firm became the largest oil company in Russia. At 50, Sechin, who served as a KGB operative in Africa, is seen as a man on the move; a crafty operator that popularized the notion that Russia would not take the Western road to development but rather one consistent with its unique history, culture, and immense size. Most recently, Mayor Sergei Sobyanin has been touted as a likely future president, many Russians noting that Yeltsin took that road to power decades ago.

Whoever replaces Putin, his successor is likely to falter for much the same reason that Gorbachev did a generation ago if the successor attempts to manage the emerging crisis within the prevailing political and economic order and not acknowledge that it has to be scrapped in favor of pluralistic economic and political institutions that are in keeping with the 21st century. The best and brightest in Russia favor a Western road to development, and, while they may be neutralized at present, ultimately they will be successful in moving Russia toward the European norm of governance.

The campaign to stabilize Russia through a police state will ultimately fail as it fosters a split among the power elite, the resurrection of the democratic movement, and massive expressions of disgruntlement on the part of ordinary Russians. But here is a pathway to either the "best" or the "worst" case scenarios. In the first case, the reactionaries are swept from power and Russia takes The Western Path to Development.

Of course, the Siloviki's failure to stabilize the country may precipitate a second outcome where the center does not hold and Russia is consumed with violent outbreaks and balkanization as disparate regional elites create de facto sovereign fiefdoms—in a word, it is stricken by all infirmities associated with the Russia in Chaos scenario.

As the U.S. Government considers the plausibility of a rebalance in relations with Russia, it behooves American strategists to pay serious attention to all of these outcomes. In particular, they cannot discount a replay of the events that led to the breakup of the Soviet Empire in 1991, only this time with an even more daunting outcome. This is not the most likely scenario, but it is certainly the most perilous one.

Russia Must Remain a Central Preoccupation of U.S. Foreign Policy.

Russia remains vital to U.S. national security for a variety of reasons:

- It alone has the capacity to destroy the United States in a nuclear war; it has 1,499 deployed warheads and 491 deployed delivery systems.

By contrast, China only has 50 intercontinental ballistic missiles that can reach the United States.[46] Russia's nuclear arsenal — tactical and strategic — and a massive inventory of chemical agents and biologic weapons constitute a prize for rogue states and terrorists of all stripes.

- Russia occupies the largest land mass of any state. Within and adjacent to its borders, where more than half of the world's population resides, there lies a vast supply of the earth's resources, including large amounts of hydrocarbon and a system of pipelines that deliver them to consumers in Europe and Asia. It has an enormous amount of minerals, critical metals, and fresh water, not to mention access to the Arctic's treasure trove of natural resources.

- Russia has made an impressive contribution to world culture, and today it is home for millions of highly educated and technologically gifted citizens. Their enterprise and talent will eventually set Russia on a firm path to modernization and enable it once again to become a significant force in world affairs.

- Russia has a UN veto, and, through a host of other international organizations and international experts, it has the means to influence events worldwide. It has been active in projecting its power in the former Soviet space, and this is the basis for Secretary Clinton's claim that Putin wants to "re-Sovietize the region" through "the guise of regional cooperation."[47] A democratic, prosperous and stable Russia will have a positive impact upon all of the countries that once were associated with the USSR.

- Arguably, the prospect of stabilizing Eurasia and much of the Greater Middle East without Russia's cooperation is well-nigh impossible.
- Russia is an Asian power, and American analysts cannot ignore it in the Asian Pivot. Were it to join China in a military alliance, the consequence for U.S. security would be immense. Conversely, harmonious Chinese-Russian-U.S. relations would enhance the international community's capacity to exploit untapped resources and promote the peace in the Far East.

The Long-Term Goal of a Re-Balance In Relations: Russia's Integration into the Euro-Atlantic Community.

After the Soviet Union imploded, the West's biggest mistake was not integrating Russia into a range of Euro-Atlantic institutions. After the Warsaw Treaty Organization had vanished, NATO's number one priority was to offer membership to former Soviet Satellites and Republics that wanted to join the alliance. At this juncture, the prospect of including Russia in this historical campaign was simply too daunting to contemplate.

Russian analysts claimed Yeltsin's biggest mistake was to ape the West and not to follow a path consistent with Russian history and culture. In response, Stephen Kotkin has observed they, ". . . seem not to have noticed that, for the most part, Russia did just that." In absence of modern democratic political institutions, such as "a strong judiciary to enforce the rule of law, property rights and the accountability of officials," Russia's plight was largely of its own making.[48]

In 1997, the NATO-Russian Joint Council was created to provide Russia with a voice in Euro-Atlantic security affairs, and similar measures followed without any substantive outcome.[49] After Bush scrapped the Cold War era ABM Treaty, Putin concluded that the window of cooperation was closing quickly, although he allowed Medvedev to explore a new relationship with the West. In 2008, Medvedev proposed a European security system that would include Russia, but it was ignored by the West and Putin was not enthusiastic about the proposal, either.

With the onset of the Obama administration, both sides agreed upon a reset in relations that led to the New Start Treaty and expansion of the Northern Distribution Network (NDN). But Putin concluded that Obama was as reluctant as Bush to provide Russia with a real voice in the proposed East European anti-missile system, and he persisted in Washington's campaign to achieve regime change in Russia. Henceforth Putin embarked upon his anti-NGO drive, ousted USIA, shut down American radio projects, and nullified the Nunn-Lugar initiative. He also accelerated his efforts to re-integrate Belarus, Moldova, and Ukraine into Russia's orbit, and to convince Georgia that the price for joining the West would prove more costly than the benefits involved. He adopted an attitude that the Americans needed him more than he needed them.

Putin did not lose sleep over the reset's demise since he reasoned the United States was in retreat internationally, while its political system was dysfunctional and the economic prospects for Obama's second term were problematic. American military might was second to none, but the Pentagon was discombobulated after a series of setbacks in the Greater Middle

East. While lecturing Russia on military reform, the Americans were indifferent to a stunning revelation: The world's only superpower could not decisively defeat opponents only armed with assault rifles and homemade bombs. In private, even U.S. analysts anticipated the fragmentation of both Iraq and Afghanistan and feared al-Qaeda-like jihadists would exploit the Syrian civil war to expand their outreach in the Islamic world.[50]

Was it any wonder that the American public complained about a huge defense budget? The Pentagon was now operating in a strange new world where it had to fight for its budget in earnest. Even Republicans with their eyes on the White House in 2016, like Kentucky Senator Rand Paul, openly disparaged a "militaristic" approach to foreign policy. Prominent defense analysts that had consulted with the Department of Defense (DoD) for decades joined the chorus of detractors. One wrote:

> It is time to abandon the United States' hegemonic strategy and replace it with one of restraint. . . . It would mean removing large numbers of U.S. troops from forward bases, and creating incentives for allies to provide for their own security.[51]

While Putin took comfort in declining American power, he resented U.S. efforts to foster regime change in much of the world, including Russia. As a former American ambassador to Ukraine opined:

> . . . his comments suggest he does not see the upheavals that swept countries such as Georgia, Ukraine, Tunisia or Egypt as manifestations of popular discontent but instead believes they were inspired, funded and directed by Washington. This may seem like a para-

noiac view, but Mr. Putin has made so many allusions to it that it is hard to conclude that he does not believe it."[52]

Today foreign policy experts within the Capital Beltway are preoccupied with Asia and are divided over the wisdom of striving for a re-balance in relations with Russia but this is not necessarily the view of the Obama administration. At the 2013 Munich Security Conference, Vice-President Joseph Biden said President Obama is convinced that "Europe is the cornerstone of our engagement with the rest of the world" and "the catalyst for our global cooperation. Europe is America's largest economic partner, to the tune of over $600 billion" and that relationship sustains jobs on both sides of the Atlantic. Anne-Marie Slaughter, a former Obama State Department official has observed, "Together, Europe and the U.S. account for more than 50% of global GDP, have the largest military force in the world by many multiples, and control a growing proportion of global energy reserves."[53]

Conversely, should the EU fragment, the implications for U.S. security are monumental, and even assuming that does not happen, U.S. planners cannot ignore the impact that Europe's protracted economic difficulties will have upon NATO. Washington is pressing its European allies to sustain the level of defense spending that they have pledged to uphold, but few have and most of them will not honor that pledge until the economic crisis in Europe is over. That may take years.

Take, for example, the case of France. It has one of Europe's most seasoned and capable military establishments—one that had demonstrated in Libya and Mali that it is prepared to deploy boots on the ground and not just "talk the talk." But hampered by slow growth and surging unemployment, it broke its pledge to the EU to hold its budget deficit to 3 percent; by the spring of 2013, it was about 3.7 percent. France has a military force of 228,000, but economic constraints will compel it to cut military personnel by 10,000, to reduce its rapid deployment force by 15,000, and to scrap its plans to construct a second aircraft carrier, as a consequence of a declining equipment budget.[54] In the meantime, what does this mean for NATO and for U.S. defense planning in Europe? Recall that after the Europeans stumbled in the former Yugoslavia, the United States was compelled to intervene to end the "Balkan Wars" that had resulted in 200,000 deaths. Had the United States been out of the picture in 2008, it is conceivable that the Russians would have snubbed the Europeans and marched onto Tbilisi, Georgia, where a puppet Russian government would have been installed.

Then, too, if the European project is stricken by serious internal political disputes — in addition to economic stagnation — what would this mean for U.S.-Russian relations? There is no easy answer to these questions, but one thing is clear: One does not have to be an alarmist to predict that the plight of the EU project and the Eurozone could culminate in serious geo-political instability on the continent. Furthermore, neither the Russian nor the Western side can unilaterally resolve outstanding security problems in Europe; they must cooperate to stabilize the continent in spite of their clashing interests and values just as great powers have done over the past several centuries.

Zbigniew Brzezinski believes the Asian Pivot is justified, but he insists that we must reaffirm our ties to Europe and that endeavor is senseless without Russia's participation. As this monograph has demonstrated, the greatest challenges to the peace in Europe are associated with dislocations associated with the collapse of European communism. As long as Russia remains outside of the major Euro-Atlantic security complex, Europe will be unstable, and that holds double should the EU and Russia suffer serious deterioration simultaneously. As the United States makes readjustments in the character and scope of its security community, it must think in terms of partnerships and joint ventures.[55]

To find a place in a Western security system, Russia must meet a host of requirements that justify this daunting undertaking; for example, reforms in the military that are germane to Russia's security challenges and consistent with a pluralistic society. In this connection, consider the following:

- A volunteer force must be established that replaces one served by draftees. There are a number of arguments against a military that depends largely upon conscripts. Among other drawbacks, 1 year is not sufficient time for recruits to acquire the skills required to operate a hi-tech force.
- An army that relies heavily upon mass mobilization of reservists and huge general purpose forces must be scrapped in favor of one with a smaller, more mobile force that is operable with air and naval units. As the Five-Day War indicated, even more important than weapons, Russia's military desperately needs to upgrade its command, control, communications, and information network.
- Much of the savings that will occur with a drawdown to a total of 700,000 soldiers can be used to attract quality personnel and provide

a professional force and their families with decent pay and housing so that they can live in dignity.

- With a lighter, more mobile, hi-tech force, Russia can address its most likely threats. For example, in ". . . the Caucasus region and the regions adjacent to the Russian-Kazakh and Russian-Chinese borders, and also along the border with North Korea."[56] It can move in this "revolutionary" direction secure in the knowledge that it retains its ace in the hole—the world's second largest nuclear strike force.
- A smaller military will provide noncommissioned officers and general officers with access to educational opportunities that better enable them to cope with a complicated global environment traumatized by turbulence.
- All of this rests upon a democratic political system whose leaders adhere to a policy of transparency.

At present, hardliners in the military-industrial complex oppose most of these items and continue to favor a military more in keeping with one following the Soviet model. If Russia goes down this road, vast sums of money will be spent on a force structure that has been overtaken by global events. More rational members of the defense establishment, however, may prevail and adopt reforms more in keeping with the prevailing strategic environment. This outcome depends upon the Russian people and their leaders, but in the meantime, there are a host of security issues that offer U.S.-Russian cooperation and can serve as confidence-building measures.

Before discussing them, one final observation bearing on any Western effort to create a new security system in the Euro-Atlantic community, with Russian participation, must be stressed. Any effort must rest on a set of firm principles. Among others, no member will claim special spheres of influence; all countries will be free to choose their security preferences; and the United States and major West European countries must reassure former Soviet entities in Central and Eastern Europe that they will continue to receive protection under Article Five of the Rome Treaty.

The Short Term Prospects For a Re-Balance in U.S.-Russian Relations.

Officials in both Moscow and Washington have discarded the word "reset," and it appears that the word "re-balance" has taken its place. Presumably this reformulation entails cautious ad hoc cooperation and reciprocal concessions. The following represents an agenda for such cooperation.

Moving Beyond the New Start Treaty.

As President Obama began his second term in office, the world was stunned by news that North Korea had detonated a nuclear weapon with greater punch than previous tests suggested. That revelation and Iran's bid for a nuclear arsenal underscored why it is in the national interest of America and Russia to keep the "nuclear genie in the bottle."

But there appear to be differences of opinion in the Kremlin. Specifically, Russian defense analysts reject Obama's long-term goal—articulated in 2009 in Prague, Czech Republic—that ultimately nuclear weapons must be eliminated. Some argue to the contrary and favor procurement of new advanced nuclear weapons and more sophisticated ICBMs not only to checkmate the West, but China as well. It remains to be seen whether their policies prevail since the costs involved are significant, and they cannot ignore the devastating price that the Soviets paid during the Cold War to keep pace with the United States.

Moving forward with the New Start agreement is a complicated endeavor, but one thing is clear: To maintain the U.S. and Russian nuclear forces on a Cold War footing is both nonsensical and dangerous. It is irrational, since neither side has any intention of launching a nuclear strike against the other one, and perilous because with nuclear weapons on an alert status in keeping with Cold War tensions, they may be launched inadvertently as a consequence of a horrible mistake or technological glitch.

Finding a Solution to the Anti-Missile Defense Conundrum.

Putin is convinced that the United States is committed to a very dangerous proposition: absolute security. Recall that Soviet strategists feared President Reagan's Strategic Defense Initiative was designed to nullify a Soviet second strike, and some Russian defense analysts see the U.S. ballistic missile defense activity in this light today. They have focused on "Phase 4 of the missile defense program in Europe, which envisions the deployment of advanced SM-3 Block IIB interceptors in Poland by 2022."[57] Moscow scoffs at the notion that this project is designed for Iranian, not Russian, ICBMs, nor do Russian analysts take comfort in claims that the United States is no threat to them.

In their defense, they can cite a prominent American student of deterrence who has observed, "In contrast to the Cold War, it is now hard to make the case that Russia is more a threat to NATO than the reverse."[58]

But demands that Russia be provided with a treaty and not a political agreement that promises the United States will not target its nuclear strike force is asking too much of Obama. That is one red line that no American President can cross at this time. Should an agreement take place, one wonders whether Russia will scrap its threat to build up its strategic offensive capabilities to counter the American missile system. It may be a bogus threat, but if it is acted upon, it would create another barrier to cooperation and produce a disastrous economic outcome for Russia.

High level discussion among U.S. and Russian officials in the spring of 2013 indicated that both sides believed the prospects for an agreement had improved, and, with two scheduled talks between Obama and Putin that year, there was hope that at long last a deal might be in the works. By the summer's end, most analysts took a much less optimistic view.[59]

Working toward a Successful U.S. Exit from Afghanistan.

From the outset of military operations in Afghanistan, Russia provided intelligence, equipment, and air and land corridors that enabled U.S. forces to project power in that country. Even more significant, Russia, through its good offices, encouraged the fighters aligned with the Northern Alliance to provide the bulk of the boots on the ground in deposing the Taliban and defeating al-Qaeda in the 2003 war.

Russia has played a pivotal role in providing the U.S. and ISAF units with a supply route—the NDN—

that has proven to be crucial. At one point, it was the only land route available when the Pakistanis closed the Karachi to Afghanistan corridor in protests over drone strikes and other U.S. operations in their country. The NDN corridor will prove critical once the allied troops exit Afghanistan to comply with the 2014 deadline. They will take 70,000 vehicles and 120,000 shipping containers with them, and it is expected that a considerable part of this massive shipment will pass through the NDN. Of course, it is conceivable that the route through Pakistan will be closed, and all of the material will have to take the northern route.[60]

Beyond that date, Russia will play a critical role when it and other stakeholders—China, India, Iran, Pakistan, and the United States—provide funding to pacify and develop a post-American Afghanistan.[61] Moscow fears drug dealers, jihadists, and criminal gangs will use Afghanistan as a pathway into Central Asia and eventually Russia, so it has incentives that exceed those in Washington to remain engaged in this turbulent region. Conversely, this troubled area is far from the United States and, in reducing its profile in the Greater Middle East, it is a candidate for exclusion.

Addressing Europe's Troubled Neighborhood.

Countries once part of the Soviet Union represent a host of different categories. For the most part, those in Eastern Europe are success stories. Some, like the Baltic democracies, are members of the EU or NATO or both, and they are politically stable and show considerable economic promise. Others have taken backward steps, like Hungary, which is displaying autocratic tendencies, or Bulgaria and Romania that are experiencing serious economic difficulties. Then there are "unaffiliated" countries that are unstable and potential flashpoints of East-West conflict. Georgia is mentioned in this connection along with Armenia, Azerbaijan, Belarus, Moldova, and Ukraine. In addition to the friction associated with the Five-Day War—and failure to resolve it and the fate of Abkhazia and South Ossetia—Azerbaijan and Armenia are on the brink of another war over Nagorno-Karabakh that could involve Turkey, which supports the former, and Russia, which supports the latter. At the same time, Lukashenka's dictatorship in Belarus is a source of friction with Lithuania and Poland, while disputes between ethnic Russians and Ukrainian nationalists represent a division that has potential for serious turbulence in Ukraine.

To prevent these latent violent conflicts from becoming manifest, Cold War protocols like the Conventional Forces in Europe Treaty (CFE) and Organization for Security Cooperation in Europe Treaty (OSCE) must be replaced by arms control and crisis management mechanisms that reflect the current strategic environment.

Syria and Iran.

The outcome of the Syrian Civil War will profoundly shape U.S.-Russian relations; as of 2013 and against the backdrop of chemical weapons use, the picture looked grim. Kremlin officials cited it as the latest example of Washington's obsession with regime change and evidence that the Obama administration had ignored lessons from Iraq. According to Sergei Karaganov, a leading foreign policy expert close to the Kremlin, "The invasion of Iraq was doomed from the outset. . . ." Moreover:

Intervention in a pre-feudal society under the banner of spreading democracy was an idea so insane that conspiracy theorists were not alone in attempting to find some covert intentions behind it.[62]

More recently, things went from bad to worse when the "West up-ended dictatorships in Tunisia, Libya and Egypt."[63]

For Putin, Assad is a loyal ally, a good customer for Russia's military hardware, and at Tartus, Syria has provided the Russian Navy with its only Mediterranean base. Diplomacy, not war, is the only solution to the conflict, but Washington has chosen the latter option. It will end badly for all concerned. Consider Obama's reluctance to intervene militarily — he fears jihadists close to al-Qaeda will be the beneficiaries, and officials in the Kremlin are of the same opinion.

In turn, American commentators have portrayed Putin's unstinting support for the Syrian dictator as irrational since Assad's "days are numbered." Putin has been impervious to the warning that his propping up of Assad has alienated Sunnis who represent about 85 percent of the world's Muslims. Looking at Syria from the perspective of Russia's long-term interest, Putin has adopted a posture that he will someday regret. The Sunnis will not forget that he not only provided Assad with weapons and diplomatic cover, he also worked with the Shiite Mullahs in Tehran to help an evil dictator wage a war against his own people that by June of 2013 amounted to 100,000 deaths.

Russian officials retort that those urging U.S. military intervention are the irrational ones and clearly victims of the American disease: "hubris." As the 2-year war has demonstrated, the jihadists may be the most likely winners, not Assad's moderate opponents.

With his downfall, al-Qaeda will secure another base to conduct its evil business in a region both strategically important to Russia and America. Furthermore, fanatical jihadists are certain to look beyond Syria as such and hope to precipitate a sectarian war throughout the region. For its part, Moscow can expect some of the Chechens, Ingush, Dagestanis, and Ossetians fighting Assad's force in Syria to join their counterparts in the North Caucasus and to carry jihad into Russia proper.[64]

It is imperative that the United States, Russia, the Arab League, the EU, and the UN prepare for the final act in the Syrian crisis before, and not after, it occurs. All have a vested interest in planning for a post-Assad government that includes a broad cross section of Syrian society, including some members of the military and government—with whom Moscow enjoys a close relationship—and the country's minorities. To wait until the fighting stops may be too late, for by then sectarian hatred will obviate any judicious outcome, and the resulting mayhem is likely to impose severe strains upon the leadership in Washington and Moscow.

Like Syria, the outcome of the Iranian crisis can have profound implications for a re-balance. Its resolution would significantly improve the prospects for cooperation on a host of other issues. A military confrontation can be avoided if Tehran shutters the Fordo enrichment plant and pledges not to enrich its uranium stockpile beyond 20 percent, excepting for a small amount to be devoted to medical purposes. In turn, sanctions that Iran is enduring would end.

Today, evidence of discord within Iranian ruling circles revolve around whether or not to strike a deal with the international community. The bite of sanctions is a major incentive and so is the prospect of a war. Then, too, should Assad be ousted from power, one of Iran's major allies would vanish and provide further support for the pragmatists who argue that international trends are not favorable to Iran and the Mullahs must make a deal with the international community.

With the election of Hassan Rouhani as president in the summer of 2013, some observers in Iran and the West believed him when he said that he was prepared to negotiate a settlement to the "nuclear crisis" with the international community. Others remained doubtful that he could do so, given the capacity of the hardliners in Tehran to subvert him.

U.S.-Russian cooperation in resolving the Iranian crisis would help stabilize the Arab-Iranian Middle East and do the same thing for a post-U.S. Afghanistan. Of greatest significance, it would avoid a war that, whatever the outcome, will not serve U.S. national security interests. Also, Iran along with Russia, China, India, and Pakistan are all stakeholders whose cooperation is essential if Afghanistan is to escape a civil war similar to the one that resulted after the Soviets left the country in the late-1980s. Although the Iranians have supported the Taliban to make mischief for Washington, they have no love for Sunni jihadists that are tormenting their Hazara-Shiite brothers in that country. Furthermore, a Taliban victory would guarantee a hostile Afghanistan on their eastern border. To take this train of events even further, resolution of the Iranian crisis would ameliorate Iranian-Saudi enmity and reduce fears of the "Iranian revolution" in other Sunni countries. It might also promote a peaceful outcome to the Israeli-Palestinian crisis and help stabilize Lebanon.

There are many analysts who reject any effort to acknowledge Iran as a major player, given the Mullahs' horrible human rights record and Iran's aggressive behavior in the vital Gulf Region.[65] But in today's turbulent global environment, no country has sufficient power to achieve its goals unilaterally and that necessitates partnerships with other countries, including those with different value systems. Curiously, the same observers that deem it realistic to engage China somehow draw a line when it comes to Tehran. Strict adherence to this double standard does not serve the vital interests of the United States. That said, the hardliners in Iran may prevail, and their success does not bode well for cooperation with them on security matters.

Cooperation in the Arctic and Northeast Asia.

Even under strained relations, the United States and allies with Arctic territory should cooperate with Russia in exploiting the vast resources that exist there and in Northeast Asia. It is imperative that they develop ground rules for development and settle points of friction before major campaigns are conducted by the member countries to exploit the untapped wealth that exists in this area of the world.

Don't Forget Russia Is an Asian Power.

Russia's Far East holds a vast storehouse of gas, oil, timber, minerals, water, and expanding trade routes. But it is thinly populated, so it needs outside help to develop resource-rich Siberia. This means close cooperation with China, Japan, and South Korea since they are major players in Northeast Asia and represent over 20 percent of global GDP. Here, then, is the answer to the question that has beguiled Russia's rulers for centuries: "How to develop its vast area east of Lake Baykal that only is home for 6 percent of Russia's population?"[66] Given its proximity, size, economic heft, and shared communist patrimony, China will play a special role in this enterprise.

The two giants share a 3,600-kilometers-long border, and trade between them amounted to $83 billion in 2012; that figure will get larger over time. China relies heavily upon Russia's hydrocarbon wealth, and that relationship will continue even as other sources of gas and oil become available. China possesses the financial resources to fund a host of investments in Russia and to capitalize joint ventures critical to both countries. It has arranged a $30 billon dollar loan for Rosneft and will be repaid with oil.

"Russia is on a course to send an unprecedented 25 percent of its crude exports to eastern markets by 2015."[67] It will be facilitated by expansion of the East Siberian-Pacific Ocean pipeline (ESPO). Presently, disputes over prices have obstructed a truly comprehensive strategic energy relationship, but there are signs that a breakthrough is in the cards.

Like their colleagues in Moscow, the Chinese believe the Americans are bent on regime change in China. PLA commanders see the United States as a threat and resent Washington's siding with Beijing's rivals in Asia—Japan, the Philippines, Taiwan, and Vietnam—over possessions in the East and South China Sea and consulting with them on security cooperation. In response, they have subverted U.S. attempts to punish Syria and Iran through UN resolutions.

China has expressed misgivings about Washington's plans to upgrade its anti-missile capability in the

Far East to address the threat from North Korea. Likewise, the PLA leadership is wary of the Americans' Asian Pivot, for they see it as part of Washington's campaign to secure permanent bases in Central Asia and to feed fears of Chinese hegemony among countries throughout the Far East.[68]

These factors and a show of autocratic solidarity may explain why Russia was the first country that Xi Jinping visited as China's new president. In a written statement upon arriving in Moscow, Xi indicated "China will make developing relations with Russia a priority in its foreign policy orientation."[69]

But while Putin talks about strategic cooperation with China, Russian defense analysts have cause to be worried. Given China's economic and demographic advantages, Russia may have to accept the role of junior partner in the relationship in spite of its vast advantage in nuclear weapons. Likewise, it is troubling to the Russian military that, while less than 10 million Russian citizens reside in the country's empty Far Eastern provinces, 120 million enterprising Chinese, who are anxious to gain access to Siberia's vast wealth, live to the south of them. Moscow has not been happy about Beijing's exploiting its economic heft to elbow aside Russia in the five Central Asian countries that formerly were Soviet Republics. Simultaneously, funding for the PLA has been significantly upgraded, and, while it has conducted maneuvers with Russian troops, both sides maintain a high state of military readiness along their common border.

Western defense analysts eagerly share these observations with their Russian counterparts to underscore their claim that Russia has no reason to fear the United States but ample cause to be nervous about the awakened giant to its south. Russian officials dismiss the warning that they face a yellow invasion. What is more, the Chinese economic miracle is helping Russia develop its Far Eastern territories via capital, trade, and parallel infrastructure programs — namely highways, rail lines, and power grids in less developed parts of Northeast Asia. In the meantime, China and Russia hope to nullify America's global influence by working with the BRIC countries, although the Brazilians and the Indians may not cooperate — this is especially true of New Delhi since it still sees China as its most serious competitor for influence in East Asia.

Also, there is a serious barrier to Sino-Russo cooperation in the foreign policy realm: China deems a stable relationship with the United States as its principle foreign policy objective. That conviction provides a window of opportunity for Washington to improve relations with Beijing and to provide a pathway for a triangular partnership between America, China, and Russia. But there is a major roadblock to this initiative: The Mandarins in Beijing are convinced that, the U.S. hegemon aside, China's major security problem is internal, not external. Managing world affairs is not one of China's priorities, and this explains why it often abstains in the Security Council rather than vote for or against a measure that excites other members of the Council. It also explains why gaining access to foreign markets is a priority. Economic, and not geo-political factors then, are conceivably the basis for China's new assertive territorial claims in the South China Sea.

No matter what the motive, Taiwan, Japan, Vietnam, and the Philippines are now responding with hostility to China's aggressive foreign policy initiatives and threats. Its highly publicized cyber attacks upon U.S. interests certainly have damaged its reputation among the American public.

Still, China has joined the United States and Russia in the most sweeping attempt to sanction Pyongyang for its recent nuclear weapons test and for selling nuclear weapons grade material to third parties. The leadership in Beijing displayed anger when their Korean cousins nullified the 60-year-old peace treaty that ended the Korean conflict. The Western media also highlighted the comments of Deng Yuwen, a deputy editor of the Communist Party publication, when he wrote in the *Financial Times*, "Beijing should give up on Pyongyang and press for the reunification of the Korean Peninsula."[70]

The sanctions upon Kim Jung-Un's government will have an economic and diplomatic impact if they are fully implemented by China. That caveat is noteworthy since China watchers observe that the Chinese leadership has not been twisting the young dictator's arms lest they produce their worst fear: the collapse of the communist regime in Pyongyang. In addition to the flight of millions of North Korean immigrants into China, it would have to live with a unified Korea allied with the United States. For PLA commanders, reunification is unthinkable, and the same holds true for their civilian masters since soon after Yuwen's op-ed was published, he was fired.

Nonetheless, should Un remain in power, the Chinese leaders must fear his reckless behavior will provoke two disturbing outcomes: First, since the February 12, 2013, detonation of an upgraded North Korean nuclear weapon, there has been a dramatic spike in the number of South Koreans, about 65 percent, who believe the time has come for them to develop their own nuclear strike force. In addition to the threat from the North, many Korean commentators believe that the U.S. pledge to provide their country with a nuclear umbrella is no longer credible, so they must build their own nuclear deterrent, or, at the very least, the Americans must return the nuclear weapons that they withdrew from South Korea in 1991.

Second, those in Tokyo who have been lobbying for a constitutional revision that would allow Japan to secure its own nuclear arsenal are now receiving a more congenial reception. Chinese strategists must conclude therefore that, if Washington dissuades Japan from taking this provocative action, in compensation the United States will have to upgrade its military presence dramatically in and around the Korean Peninsula.

In response to mounting concern about North Korea, high level American and Chinese officials have been conducting talks — including communications between both presidents — to reduce both provocative words and actions on the part of the United States and North Korea. In June 2013, President Obama and President Xi Jinping met in the Californian desert to discuss the future of U.S.-China relations. No concrete agreements were reached, but both presidents clearly indicated that, in spite of outstanding areas of dispute, they agreed it was in the vital interest of both countries to stop the slide in relations. That said, neither man seemed to have any idea about how that goal could be achieved, given Beijing's concern about the Asian pivot and Washington's concern about China's aggressive posture toward its neighbors — some of whom are U.S. allies.[71]

The prospects for more harmonious relations between China and the United States received a body blow several weeks later when it was revealed by an American contractor working for the intelligence community that Washington had monitored communications from China with special intent. To make matters worse, the young man in question, Edward Snowden, originally sought refuge in Hong Kong, which he threatened to use as a base to disseminate top secret material collected by the National Security Agency. He then fled to Moscow in transit to a safe harbor somewhere in the world, and that incident provided a further chill to American-Russian relations. At the same time, many foreign policy analysts predicted that this affair would bring both Russia and China closer together in the face of the "American" threat to their security.

In assessing the relationship between China, Russia, and the United States, the following questions are pertinent: What are the prospects for a close Sino-Russian security condominium? Is a U.S.-Russian security relationship possible? What are the chances for a triangular relationship that promotes the security interests of all three parties? One thing is clear on all of these matters: the nature of American-Russian relations could have an impact upon the future of Washington's Asian pivot. In considering the pivot, then, the U.S. defense community must include Russia in their assessments of the security environment in Asia.

Now Is Not the Time for a Pause.

The Syrian crisis provides overwhelming evidence that there is no justification for a pause in attempts to sustain U.S.-Russian security cooperation. Even if efforts to negotiate a settlement to the crisis fail and prospects for cooperation take a nosedive in the short run, in the long run, both Obama and Putin recognize that they must remain engaged.

Of course, the road ahead will be difficult. Ever since Putin's crackdown and the Magnitsky-Litvinov imbroglio—the U.S. law that punishes Russian human rights violators in the first case and the Russian law in response that denies Americans the right to adopt Russian orphans in the second one—some in Washington have recommended a pause in U.S.-Russian relations. They claim that in this frigid environment, fruitful cooperation is a nonstarter, but they should recall that the golden era of arms control occurred in the midst of the Cold War and at a time when the Soviet Union was called "the evil empire." In 1987, the author of these words, Ronald Reagan, negotiated the elimination of an entire category of rockets through the Intermediate Range Nuclear Forces (INF) Treaty with Mikhail Gorbachev. It was facilitated over a period of years by the interaction of mid-level diplomats and the cooperation of military representatives on both sides. This interaction promoted confidence and trust and resulted in a number of arms control agreements that served U.S. security.

Convinced that Russia has no choice but to engage the West, Putin appears ready to reaffirm cooperation with Obama on an ad hoc basis, although he will prove to be a difficult partner since he is preoccupied with consolidating his power at home and sees value in taking a hard line with Washington in that enterprise. At the same time, Putin understands that it is neither in his interest nor that of Russia to turn his back on the world's only superpower. He also knows that many of those in the United States that are bitter political opponents of Obama favor confrontational relations with Moscow. In sum, he has 3 years to reach an accommodation with the United States.

From the American perspective, cooperating with Russia on security matters is one step in many that some U.S. statesmen hope will secure Russia's cooperation in addressing common security problems — the proliferation of WMD, the radical jihadist threat, and many other issues. Also, U.S. proponents of the reset — or whatever is the current terminology — hope that ultimately it will lead to a security partnership between Russia and the Euro-Atlantic community. Of course, it will be a long-term effort, and it will take patience to accomplish. It certainly will be sidetracked by intervening events but, if fruitful, it will enhance U.S. security by establishing a more stable foothold in Europe and provide a foundation upon which Washington's Asian pivot will rest.

The Boston Marathon bombings have given a positive boast to the prospects for more extensive American-Russian cooperation in joint anti-terrorist operations. In the immediate aftermath of that tragedy, many Russian officials welcomed comments from American analysts and diplomats regarding insurgencies in the North Caucasus. Perhaps even more significant, many ordinary Americans for the first time were informed that the Russians were helping the United States in the fight against Islamic jihadists — the very same people responsible for 9/11. In sum, there is a basis for the claim that U.S.-Russian cooperation in fighting terrorism is plausible.

This does not mean ignoring human rights violations in Russia, but it means treating the regime there the same way Washington treats the Chinese ruling elite. U.S. and Russian leaders must not waste time but work toward a peaceful resolution of the crises in Syria, Iran, and North Korea. Not to do so is to run the risk of watching latent disasters become manifest calamities that will do grave harm to the security of their respective countries.

The uncertain outcome of the Syrian civil war has the potential to sabotage even a limited security relationship, but proponents of this initiative cite a meeting of the minds on an important matter: preventing the Syrian crisis from morphing into a horrendous regional disaster. Russian commentators, for example, have taken comfort in the belief that Putin's arguments are having some impact upon Western analysts and statesmen.

As Pavel Baev states:

> What adds credibility to the Russian leadership's case, at least in their own eyes, is the supposition that only violent chaos and state failure can follow the collapse of the al-Assad regime. Every month of the civil war makes this more plausible. As the internecine fighting escalates, the rebel groups and factions inevitably grow more radicalized. . .,[72]

and this development has caused expressions of concern in Israel since it "must take into account the prospect of an Islamic state emerging in Syria."[73] In sum, Putin clearly relishes the notion that the Americans have had to concede that his claim that the international campaign to dump Assad may produce a worse outcome than Assad's ouster is designed to prevent. At the same time, Russian analysts believes that the Americans simply do not understand the complexities of conflicting forces that prevail in the Greater Middle East. In short, they are victims of a major intellectual error. Putin may be kidding himself when he brushes aside the claim that his support for the Syrian dictator will cause him problems among the largely Sunni Islamic community. The same may be said for his disregarding the fact that a disaster in Syria will potentially do far greater harm to Russia's security than it will do to the United States.

Preparing for the Unexpected.

As American and Russian leaders struggle to find avenues of cooperation, history instructs them to "expect the unexpected." The Strategic Arms Limitations Treaty (SALT) II was aborted by President Carter in 1980 as a result of the Soviet invasion of Afghanistan. Some observers have mentioned this incident in pondering what role the Winter Olympics might play in U.S.-Russian relations. They will be conducted in the Russian Black Sea city of Sochi in February 2014. Open discussion of this matter surfaced when the fate of Snowden was being considered. The United States demanded that he be returned from the Russian airport where he was seeking temporary asylum to face charges that he leaked classified National Security Council (NSC) documents. Russia's refusal to comply prompted expressions of outrage at both ends of Pennsylvania Avenue. Although a lonely voice, Senator Lindsey Graham, the Republican from South Carolina, demanded the United States boycott the games in retaliation.

However, Graham identified something that Putin highly values. The Kremlin has invested $51 billion to construct a massive Winter Olympic Games complex in Sochi. Project costs may far exceed that amount since criminal gangs and corrupt officials are having a royal feast filching funds from the enterprise. Entire neighborhoods are being bulldozed while their residents are desperately searching for new shelter and a large number of workers from the impoverished Central

Asian Republics are being paid abysmally low wages to fill construction jobs. Putin has embarked upon this expensive project with one major goal in mind: to improve Russia's international image and to proclaim that it will no longer take a back seat to anyone.

His crusade, however, is not trouble-free. Sochi sits in the midst of the turbulent Caucasus, home for many disgruntled minorities. Circassian nationalists claim Sochi as part of their ancient homeland — a territory that their ancestors occupied until the early-19th century when they were expelled by Russian invaders. Like other nations in the North Caucasus seeking independence from Moscow, they may exploit the publicity surrounding Sochi to publicize their demands globally. Some of them, like Russia's most wanted terrorist — Doku Umarov — have already threatened violence to publicize their jihadist war with Russia. Presumably, this would include suicide bombings and attacks on public officials and security units, and even the athletes may become targets. Kremlin officials believe they have things under control, but they may be badly mistaken. Whatever the challenges facing them, how could the insurgents forgo a once-in-a-lifetime opportunity to make their plight known to the world in a bold terrorist strike? Of course, the global publicity spawned by the awful bombings in Boston is likely to encourage copycats to produce similar mayhem at the Sochi Olympics.

Putin's repressive crackdown may encourage liberal Russians out of desperation to seek new ways to respond to his wholesale attack upon their human rights. Some gay rights activists, for example, may endorse a campaign to boycott the Olympics. It is unlikely that athletic organizations from the participating countries, their governments, and their financial sponsors will **condone** a boycott and withdraw as many did during the 1980 Olympic Games in Moscow. President Obama has indicated that, while he finds the anti-gay campaign in Russia repugnant, he does not favor a boycott. But under existing circumstances, the threat resonates, given the dramatic technological changes that have occurred since 1980 in the information arena. In this instance, the Internet and social media make an unprecedented international political protest possible. There are thousands of people within Russia, and Russians in the diaspora, along with human rights activists in the West, who have the capacity to undertake a campaign of this nature. Also, unlike the North Caucasus insurgents, the Russian dissidents are not vulnerable to the charge that "they are nothing more than terrorists."

Even if the campaign fails to sabotage the games, it offers dissidents an international event around which they can publicize the plight of Russian democrats and do grave damage to Putin's quest to improve Russia's image globally. Likewise, Putin's crackdown could become a problem for Washington, as it has the capacity to facilitate an anti-Kremlin backlash that could make cooperation with the Russian government a truly costly political enterprise for the American government.

EPILOGUE

The Navalny Question.

By the fall of 2013, Putin-watchers concluded that Russia was already on the road to Stalin Lite. Many also believed that one could gain a glimpse of Russia's future by assessing the fate of Navalny. About a week after the Boston massacre, Navalny was tried for embezzling $500,000 from a timber company in Kirov. The charge was fabricated and driven by political considerations that emanated from Moscow since local authorities found no basis for it. By this time, the tall, blond, 37-year-old blogger was no longer a mystery man, since publicity surrounding his brave confrontation with the Kremlin had earned him the respect of a growing number of Russians. They admired his courage, shared his anger about corruption, and enjoyed his tart humor directed at the Kremlin. His nationalistic proclivities and common touch had the potential of attracting provincials to him. Two years previously, he had a name recognition of 6 percent, but by the spring of 2013, it had escalated to 47 percent.[74]

In a short period of time, he had emerged as a political opponent of consequence, and his political ambitions earned him the respect and enmity of the Kremlin overlords. As a result, he anticipated that he would be charged with a crime, found guilty, and, even if he escaped a prison sentence, his being a felon would deny him the opportunity to run for public office. On July 18, he was found guilty and received a 5-year prison sentence along with a large fine. But the very next day, he was released and was free until his appeal was considered. Some Russian watchers assumed that the Kremlin leadership was behind this move out of anticipation of a planned street protest to be conducted the following weekend. Others indicated that his release was further proof that the Putin team had been divided over how best to address the Navalny question. Some feared that if he was harshly treated, he would become a martyr. Others wanted to crush him since there were doubts about the ability of associates to continue the fight while he was in prison.

Among some prominent foreign commentators, the incident underscored a gathering consensus: Navalny had become the most effective spokesman for the anti-Putin opposition, and he had the unique personal qualifications to lead a growing army of disgruntled Russians in a truly significant political movement.

Unlike many of his cohorts, Navalny did not flee Russia but remained there prepared to continue his fight in prison with the help of his comely and articulate wife, Julia. He has stated repeatedly that the power and capacity of the Kremlin overlords had been grossly exaggerated. "The people who work in business at a high enough level can tell you that there's no machine at all." They may be able to "destroy a single person," like Khodorkovsky or himself. But they cannot do so "against a huge number of people, there's no machine. It's a ragtag group of crooks and unified under the portrait of Putin."

In a blog the day before he travelled to Kirov to attend his trial, he wrote: "Enough whining and being scared. It's time to organize and get to work." Then after comments on freedom and human rights he continued:

> All of these years, I've been learning alongside of you how to organize even in conditions of a state propaganda machine, intimidation, and a lack of money. . . . There is no one but you. There is no one who cares about what's going on in the country more than you. There are no magic volunteers who will show up and do the work for you. . . ."[75]

An intense crowd of supporters greeted him at the Moscow train station the day after he was found guilty. His return was covered via the Internet, including visual segments; even the Kremlin-dominated TV gave him coverage. Since then, Russian-watchers have concluded that he is the real deal, a man capable of leading a popular anti-Kremlin movement, even though he is someone who faces a jail sentence. He told the gathering that, in effect, they had demonstrated that there was no reason to fear the Kremlin's wrath, and they were responsible for his release.

Some pundits had a different perspective, claiming that Navalny's help was required to give legitimacy to the anticipated re-election of the acting Mayor of Moscow, Sergei Sobyanin. It was assumed that Navalny would run for that office and lose the race but in the process demonstrate that, even in a fair fight, the Kremlin-backed candidate would win. The young blogger pledged to achieve a victory for the people—his election—but the odds makers deemed that a remote prospect.

On September 9, the Kremlin was shocked by the election results: Sobyanin allegedly received 51 percent of the vote so he was re-elected without a run-off. But official results indicated that Navalny got almost one-third of the votes cast even though he did not have access to TV and was denied other assets to which the Mayor was privy. What is more, Navalny claimed that the election was fabricated, and Sobyanin did not obtain the votes required to claim a first round victory.

The blogger attracted an army of young people— "Generation Navalny"—to his campaign, ". . . the thousands of young people who came of age after the Soviet collapse and who yearn for a more inclusive politics." They conducted a ground campaign that Russians had never witnessed in their history. They "pounded the pavement, knocked on doors, passed out leaflets, manned phone lines, and organized online for the charismatic opposition leader."[76]

Navalny threatened to organize his followers in street protests, but whatever does take place, analysts have spent **considerable** time pondering the future of his movement. Did his followers have the resolve and political acumen to fill his shoes if he went to prison? Could they expand their power base? Could Navalny continue the fight from prison? Has his success inspired members of the establishment to consider an alliance with him? There are rumors that he has secret talks with some pragmatic Kremlin insiders; are they true, and, if so, what do they mean?

Although uncertain of the answers, a growing number of analysts both within and outside of Russia are convinced that Navalny's challenge is further evidence that Putin's future is in grave doubt. Indeed, some have concluded that even some of his closest associates now have reservations about his capacity to cope with his political opponents.

Whatever Navalvy's fate, as indicated earlier, the turbulence associated with the Power Vertical could conceivably produce two compelling outcomes. First, Putin's repressive measures justify the claim that he is creating a police state where the authorities intrude upon both the private and public space of the Russian people. Or second, pragmatists in the Kremlin like Sobyanin and Shoigu join forces with the new politicians as exemplified by Navalny, and together they take the measures necessary to set Russia on a slow road to pluralism.

Or perhaps there is a third outcome; Putin's worse fears are realized as Russia disintegrates after it proves incapable of addressing its cascading cultural, economic, and political problems. U.S. planners must pay serious attention to all of these questions, given Russia's large imprint on the international stage.

Syria and U.S.-Russian Relations.

On September 10, President Obama delivered a much anticipated speech on why he was prepared to punish the Syrian regime for using poison gas against its own people. But he stunned the nation when he said that he would delay taking military action. As a consequence of back-channel deliberations, a peaceful resolution of the crisis was at hand. It was called the "Russian Plan" and proposed that Syria surrender its poison gas to UN weapons inspectors for their ultimate destruction. Within a week, a number of equally unexpected developments occurred in rapid order:

- Putin scolded Obama in a *New York Times* opinion editorial for celebrating American exceptionalism. But in other remarks, Putin indicated that he trusted Obama to honor any peace initiative.
- John Kerry and Lavrov met in Geneva to begin talks about how to destroy Syria's gas arsenal.
- Assad gave impetus to their "framework agreement" by sending a letter to the UN asserting that Syria would sign the Chemical Weapons Convention.
- American and Russian diplomats established the basis for a diplomatic solution to the Syrian Civil War through the Geneva-2 peace initiative.

Critics who scoffed at the Russian Plan were shocked by these revelations and even more so when the United States accepted Moscow's demands that Washington not insert language in the UN resolution that condoned the use of force if Syria violated the agreement. Some pundits suggested that Putin had outmaneuvered Obama since the Russian Plan was a rouse designed to buy time for Assad.

Seasoned foreign policy analysts, however, indicated that Putin was genuinely concerned about Syria's toxic weapons because he feared they might be secured by jihadists who would use them in the North Caucasus. They also found reason to acknowledge that the Kremlin was justified in pressing the Americans on the legitimate question: "What would happen after Assad was removed from power?" Moscow feared Syria would collapse much like Qaddafi's Libya had but with even far worse consequences for the region.

Western leaders rightfully scolded Putin and Lavrov for suggesting that the rebels in Syria, and not Assad's forces, were responsible for the gas attacks that the weapons inspectors confirmed. Such claims in the face of overwhelming evidence to the contrary were absurd, and they diminished Putin's campaign to burnish his image as an international leader of consequence. At the same time, the international community applauded his diplomatic efforts and, in turn, enhanced his image at home. Indeed, the role he played in finding a nonviolent resolution of the Syrian crisis indicated that Russia was once again an international actor that could no longer be ignored. Russia was back! Just what that would mean for Putin over the long term, however, remained unclear. After all, Russia's most serious security problems were internal, not external.

Finally, what did this week of tumultuous events mean for a) U.S.-Russia relations and b) the U.S. national security community? In the first instance, recall that after the June G-8 Summit in Ireland, pundits in Washington claimed U.S.-Russian relations had hit an insurmountable firewall. The time had come to bury the "reset corpse," and any effort to revive it was foolhardy. But one can make the contrary case; joint efforts to resolve the Syrian Civil War suggested a dramatic new chapter in the reset was about to begin. The steps already undertaken obligated both sides to continue their collaboration. That said, the road ahead was rocky and uncertain. For example, what was to be done about the al-Qaeda fighters in Syria?

For its part, the U.S. national security community must consider a number of outcomes: a Syria without Assad but under the control of a broad but weak coalition of leaders; a country fragmented into several parts; and a Syria where jihadists are the most dominant military force. In response to these outcomes, U.S. defense analysts must assess what role American forces would play in a multilateral campaign to eliminate them and to stabilize Syria. Direct U.S. military involvement might be a bridge too far, but clearly American military assets would be required to achieve a successful international campaign.

It is premature to make any firm predictions about the fate of Geneva-2, U.S.-Russian efforts to crush the al-Qaeda groups in Syria, and the broader issue of security cooperation on their part. It is evident, however, that in spite of the many obstacles to cooperation, it is in the U.S. national interest to work with Russia where possible and address shared security concerns.

ENDNOTES

1. For an excellent political biography of Putin and the events surrounding his rise to power, see Fiona Hill and Clifford G. Gaddy, *Mr. Putin: Operative in the Kremlin*, Washington, DC: Brookings Institution Press, 2013, p. 5. For a brief but insightful assessment of Russia today, see Dmitri Trenin *et. al.*, *The Russian Awakening*, Moscow, Russia: Carnegie Moscow Center, November 2012.

2. Ben Judah, "Has the Russian opposition lost its way?" *opendemocracy.net*, November 27, 2012.

3. It is noteworthy that Russian-watchers agreed that something of significance was abroad in Russia and this included commentators close to the Kremlin.

4. In their assessment of Russia's future, Maria Lipman and Nikolay Petrov describe one likely outcome as "Russia on the way to a resurgent dictatorship — 'Stalin Lite'." See Maria Lipman and Nikolay Petrov, "Conclusions," Maria Lipman and Nikolay Petrov, eds., *Russia in 2020*, Washington, DC: Carnegie for International Peace, 2011, p. 603.

5. For a discussion of Putin's years in Dresden, see Hill and Gaddy, pp. 118-123.

6. See Joe Nocera, "The New Russian Mob," *The New York Times*, March 28, 2013.

7. For an excellent assessment of growing opposition to Putin that also provides insight into reasons why many Russians continue to support him, see Mikhail Dmitriev and Daniel Treisman, "The Other Russia: Discontent Grows in the Hinterlands," *Foreign Affairs*, September-October, 2012, pp. 59-86.

8. Kirill Rogov, "The 'third cycle': Is Russia Headed Back to the Future," Lipman and Petrov, eds., p. 125.

9. *Ibid*, p. 126.

10. There is ample evidence to explain Putin's popularity when one consults dramatic increases in wages. Over the past "decade before the global financial crisis, real household incomes rose by 140 percent." See Dmitriev and Treisman, p. 66.

11. "In 2002, the newly privatized oil companies — like Yukos and Sibneft — accounted for over 81 percent of Russian oil output." To keep the oil and gas revenues flowing, Putin struck deals with foreign oil companies and Western investors. But the international financial crisis struck Russia, and by 2009, its GDP declined by 7.8 percent. See Thane Gustafson, "Putin's Petroleum Problem," *Foreign Affairs*, November-December, 2012, p. 88.

12. Andrew E. Kramer, "Russia's Desire for Cars Grow, and Foreign Makers Take Notice," *The New York Times*, December 12, 2012.

13. Jana Kobzova and Tomas Valasek, "Putin Redux: Foreign Policy under Russia's Comeback President," Kurt Voker and Ieva Kupce, eds., *Nordic-Baltic-American Cooperation: Shaping the US European Agenda*, Washington, DC: Center for Transatlantic Relations, 2012, p. 10.

14. For a cogent discussion of Russia's energy strategy, see Keith Smith, "Unconventional Gas and European Security: Politics and Foreign Policy of Frocking in Europe," Washington, DC: Center for Strategic and International Studies, 2012.

15. In searching for the origins of Russian autocracy and imperialism, Robert D. Kaplan has provided a simple one-word answer: Geography. Putin is simply a "run-of-the-mill," Russian dictator..."whose cynical neo-imperialism are the wages of a deep, deep geographical insecurity." He is just the latest in a long line of men and women who have ruled Russia with a mailed fist because "Putin looks out in Europe and sees what the tsars and commissars saw before...a history of invasion against Russia by the Swedes, the Poles, the French, the Germans, the Lithuanians, etc. and therefore, just like the communist rulers before him, he wants buffer states." Interview: Robert D. Kaplan on How Geography Affects the Fate of Nations," *RFE/RL.org*, September 11, 2012.

16. Owen Matthews, "The End of Putinomics," *Newsweek.com*, December 30, 2012.

17. *Ibid.*

18. Paul Goble, "Russian Government Now Views internet as Main Threat to its Position," *Window on Eurasia*, February 5, 2013. It is also noteworthy that through "crowd funding," — a practice perfected by the two Obama presidential campaigns — democratic activists secured funding from ordinary people not the traditional "fat cats." For example, see Alexey Sidorenko, "Society and the State on the Internet: a Call for Change," in Lipman and Petrov, eds., p. 586.

19. Peter Pomerantsev, "2012, the year the Kremlin lost control of the script," *Opendemocracy.net*, December 28, 2012.

20. "Former Russian Finance Minister Alexei Kudrin: 'We have to Take a Chance with More Democracy'," *Der Spiegel*, January 23, 2013.

21. For an analysis of why the West will rebound, see Roger C. Altman, "Why America and Europe Will Emerge Stronger from the Financial Crisis," *Foreign Affairs*, January-February 2013, pp. 8-13.

22. For a discussion of China's future, see *Foreign Affairs*, January-February, 2013.

23. One of the most perceptive observers of Russia today has observed:

> The effectiveness of Russian soft power in the CIS could also be improved through Russian media and Russian Internet becoming acknowledged as the most reliable source of information and vehicles for the dissemination of new ideas across the entire expanse of the FSU. . . .

Needless to say, the war on the Internet and independent media outlets presently underway in Russia does grave harm to Putin's soft-power campaign. Dmitry Trenin, "Russia's Relations with the CIS Countries: Outlook for 2020," Valdai Discussion Club, April 2, 2013.

24. For example, see Lipman and Petrov, "Conclusions," pp. 593-614.

25. Will Englund, "Russia's 'Tandem' No Longer in Sync," *The Washington Post*, February 24, 2013.

26. Leon Aron, "The Putin Doctrine," *foreignaffairs.com*, March 9, 2013, p. 2.

27. Fiona Hill and Clifford Gaddy, "Dealing with the Real Putin," *The New York Times*, February 4, 2013.

28. Putin Address to the Federal Assembly, December 12, 2012, p. 10.

29. In an example of their uplifting lyrics, it was proclaimed: "We are being assaulted by the seed of the Mongol Horde, Attacked by the yoke of the infidels. But the sky of the Slavs boils in our veins."

30. For a discussion of Kaliningrad and the question of its legal status, see Richard J. Krickus, *The Kaliningrad Question*, Lanham, MD: Rowman & Littlefield, 2002. For remarks bearing on Siberia, see Paul Goble, "Despite Moscow's promises, Russia's Far East Remains 'More Dead than Alive' Experts Say," *Window on Eurasia*, December 2, 2012. He notes that "within a radius of 1,000 kilometers of Vladivostok, there live 300 million people, five times more than live within the same radius of Moscow." Moreover, the economic output of this area is three times larger than all of Russia.

31. Lyudmila Alexandrova, "With Internet gaining wide influence in Russia, authorities seek to step up control over it," Itar-Tass World Service, February 4, 2013.

32. Brian Whitmore, "The Kremlin's New Deal," *RFE/RL.org*, March 13, 2013.

33. Stephen F. Cohen, "How Obama can avert a new Cold War," *The Washington Post*, February 14, 2013.

34. Aron.

35. Putin, in his response to claims that he was attempting to "re-Sovietize" many of the USSR's former appendages, said that the former Soviet Republics enjoy a "common language, similar mindsets, as well as interconnected transportation and energy infrastructure as natural factors pushing Russian-led integration in the post-Soviet space." It is no different in this respect than the EU's integration of countries with similar common bonds. Dumitru Minzarari, "Russia is Building Diplomatic and Military Tools to Prevent Western Resistance to its Eurasian Union," *Eurasia Daily Monitor*, December 11, 2012.

36. Thomas Graham, "Russia and the World," Lipman and Petrov, eds., p. 14.

37. See, for example, Brian Whitmore, "Vladimir the Weak," *RFE/RL.org,* March 20, 2013. Paul Goble, "Having Released 'Obscurantism genie,' Putin Could Lose Control over It, Gontmakher Says," *Window on Eurasia,* February 19, 2013. Hill and Gaddy observe that one of the reasons Putin is so obsessed with the "general idea of unity and unifying" is that he sees it as an "anti-dote to collapse and disintegration." See Putin, p. 58.

38. Leonid Radzikhovsky, "Beware the apocalypse," *Russia beyond the Headlines,* July 8, 2011.

39. As far back as the early-1960s, Brzezinski cited economic, political, and social problems in the Soviet Union that would ultimately lead to its demise. In this connection, see "The Soviet Political System: Transformation or Degeneration," in his *The Dilemmas of Change in Soviet Politics,* New York: Columbia University Press, 1960, pp. 1-24.

40. See Jack F. Matlock, Jr., *Superpower Illusions,* New Haven, CT: Yale University Press, 2010, p. 87.

41. Graham, "Russia and the World," p. 10.

42. Joint Chiefs of Staff, *The National Military Strategy of the United States of America,* Washington, DC: Office of the Joint Chiefs of Staff, 2011, p. 13.

43. "Russia updates its Foreign Policy Concept," *Russia beyond the Headlines/Rossiyskaya Gazeta,* February 25, 2013.

44. For a pessimistic appraisal of the Eurasian Union, see Richard Weitz, "Global Insight: Dim Prospects for Putin's Eurasian Union," *World Politics Review,* October 11, 2011.

45. Whatever the sources, an imploded Russia will far exceed the security threat—"Global Terrorism"—that has preoccupied the U.S. military since 9/11. It has the potential of producing a geo-political disruption even more far reaching in scope and magnitude. For more on the civil war within Islam, see Richard

Krickus, "It Is a Civil War within Islam Not Global Terrorism," *e-International Relations*, June 12, 2012.

46. Walter Pincus, "To Cut the Deficit, Cut the Nuclear Arsenal." *The Washington Post*, December 13, 2012.

47. Kathy Lally, "Ties between U.S., Russia Sour," *The Washington Post*, January 14, 2013.

48. Stephen Kotkin, *Armageddon Averted: The Soviet Collapse 1970-2000*, New York: Oxford University Press, 2008, pp. 164-165. For an assessment more critical of the United States, see Stephen F. Cohen, *Soviet Fates And Lost Alternatives: From Stalinism To The Cold War*, New York: Columbia University Press, 2009.

49. For a discussion of efforts to provide Russia with a voice in European security, see Richard J. Krickus, "Russia in NATO: Thinking about the Unthinkable," Copenhager, Denmark: Danish Institute of International Affairs, 2002.

50. During the 10th anniversary of the Iraq war, there was an avalanche of articles that reassessed the war. For an American and Arab view on the event, respectively, see John A. Nagl, "What America Learned in Iraq," and Ahmad Saadawi, "A Decade Of Despair," both in the *The New York Times*, March 20, 2013.

51. Barry Pozen, "The Case for a Less Activist Foreign Policy," *Foreign Affairs*, January-February 2013, p. 118.

52. Steven Pifer, "The Future Course of the U.S.-Russia Relationship," Washington, DC: The Brookings Institution, March 21, 2012, p. 4.

53. Anne-Marie Slaughter, "The Coming American Century, the ISN Blog," March 11, 2013. Of course, a rebalance in U.S.-EU relations is complicated by Europe's ongoing economic crisis. The collapse of the financial system in Cyprus is just the latest example of the EU's precarious existence. The stock of Euro-Skeptics is on the rise while supporters of a "united Europe" are suffering at the ballot box, and separatist movements are attracting supporters in Scotland, Catalonia and parts of France and Italy, while parties with a racist agenda are ascendant in societies with large Islamic and African populations.

54. See Steven Erlanger, "Grim Economics Shape France's Military Spending," *The New York Times*, April 30, 2013.

55. Video: Zbigniew Brzezinski: Lessons from a Life in Strategy, Washington, DC: Center for Strategic and International Studies, February 20, 2013.

56. Alexander Golts, "The Armed Forces in 2020: Modern or Soviet?" in Lipman and Petrov, eds., p. 380.

57. Robert Coalson, "Explainer: What's New In U.S. Missile Defense Plans?" *RFE/RL.org,* March 18, 2013.

58. Richard K. Betts, "The Lost Logic of Deterrence," *Foreign Affairs*, March-April, 2013, p. 90. This may be a minority view among American defense analysts, but many who may reject it believe it is prudent to include Russia in the anti-missile project.

59. Will Englund, "Obama letter to Putin: Sign of a thaw?" *The Washington Post*, April 16, 2013.

60. Andrew E. Kramer, "Rumors about Uzbekistan Leaders' Health Set Off Succession Debate," *The New York Times*, April 7, 2013. For a discussion of this matter, see Richard J. Krickus, *The Afghanistan Question and the Reset in U.S.-Russian Relations*, Carlisle, PA: Strategic Studies Institute, U.S. Army War College, 2011.

61. Krickus, *The Afghanistan Question.*

62. Fyodor Lukyanov, "Russia's Place in the World of Unintended Consequence, or Murphy's Law and Order," in Lipman, ed., p. 85. At one point, Putin said that he was "not concerned with the fate of Assad's regime," and that statement appeared to have dealt a body blow to the tyrant. But later, he aborted efforts through the UN Security Council to force out Assad and continued to supply him with arms. Russian Foreign Minister Lavrov also displayed a state of confusion on Syria but later lambasted the rebels for refusing to negotiate a peace with Assad. See John Warrick and Colum Lynch, "Assad Said To Be Afraid, Isolated As Rule Fades," *The Washington Post*, December 29, 2013.

63. *Ibid.*

64. See Paul Goble, "Moscow Must Prepare for Syria-Type War in the North Caucasus, Former MVD Officer Says," *Window on Eurasia*, April 4, 2013.

65. For background to U.S.-Iranian relations, see Trita Parsi, *Treacherous Alliance*, New Haven, CT: Yale University Press, 2007.

66. Thomas Graham, "Do U.S.-Russian Relations Have a Future in Northeast Asia?" Johnson's Russia List, December 4, 2012.

67. Jake Rudnitsky, "Putin Pipeline to Send 25% of Russia's Oil Exports East," Bloomberg, March 7, 2013.

68. See Simon Saradzhyan, "Russia Needs to Develop Eastern Provinces as China Rises," *Ria Novosti*, March 5, 2013; and David M. Herszenhorn and Chris Buckley, "China's Leader Argues for Closer Ties With Russia," *The New York Times*, March 23, 2013.

69. David M. Herszenhorn and Chris Buckley, "China's New Leader, Visiting Russia, Promotes Nation's Economic and Military Ties," *The New York Times*, March 22, 2013.

70. Martin Fackler and Choe Sang-Hun, "As North Korea Blusters, South Flirts With Talk of Nuclear Arms," *The New York Times*, March 11, 2013.

71. For a brief but cogent analysis of the Obama-Xi summit, see Robert A. Manning, "Beijing and Washington Share Indeterminate Future," *The National Interest*, June 13, 2013.

72. Pavel K. Baev, "Not Everything is wrong with Russia's Syria Strategy," *PONARS Eurasia*, April 26, 2013.

73. *Ibid.*

74. "Justice in Russia: The Navalny Affair," *Economist.com*, April 20, 2013.

75. Julia Ioffe, "The Most Dangerous Blogger in the World: How Alexseu Navalny changed Russian politics," *The New Republic* online, July 18, 2013, pp. 9-11.

76. Tom Balmforth, "Generation N: How Navalny Shook Up Politics With His Army Of Volunteers," *RFE/RL.org,* September 9, 2013.